TURQUOISE INK

Photomemoirs Series - Book 2

Front cover photo:
Ruth McKenzie, aged 19, in Suez, 1951

photo**M**emoirs

This book is published by Photomemoirs.co. Anyone can write a photo memoir without any writing skills. Photomemoirs is an easy and fun way to do it. To get started, order the Photomemoirs instruction pack. Then find your most memorable photographs and record their story in your own words - as if you were showing them to someone and sharing your memories. Send us the photos and recordings and we will make your book. The concept of Photomemoirs is to be more than a photo album, but less than an autobiography. To sign up visit our website www.Photomemoirs.co

Turquoise Ink

This Photomemoirs book is by Ruth McKenzie Bird. She was born in Aberdeen in 1931 but didn't stay long enough to get to know it. An only child with a vivid imagination, she was whisked off to the Far East, caught up in the events of the Second World War, and raised to adulthood on the African continent.

She almost made it back to the UK to start a more sedate adult life there, only marriage to a young army officer put paid to that...

Ruth wrote about her peripatetic life in her trademark turquoise ink, hence the name of this book, and we - her family - think that you might enjoy the funny and frank observations that she wrote about as much as we have.

In loving memory of Ruth, Dickie and Anne

Contents

Introduction

Ruth was born in Aberdeen, Scotland in 1931, to Ethel and Ronald McKenzie, a petroleum oil engineer with Royal Dutch Shell.

Ruth (aged 18 months) and her father Ronald McKenzie:
Scotland, summer 1933

In 1936, when Ruth was five years old, she and her mother sailed to Southeast Asia on the P&O ocean liner RMS (Royal Mail Ship) *Corfu* to join her father in British Borneo. They stopped at Marseilles and Port Said before entering the Suez Canal, which links the Mediterranean to the Red Sea.

RMS Corfu 1932. Picture by Allan C. Green 1878 - 1954 - State Library of Victoria

They were still cruising south down the Suez Canal when Ruth celebrated her sixth birthday: as she rushed out on deck to thank her friends in the ship's crew for their birthday card, a gust of wind whipped the card out of her hand and deposited it in the water far below them. Little Ruth was startled, but the crew turned it into a huge joke and they all hung over the railings to wave goodbye to the card until it disappeared. The ship eventually exited the canal at Suez and continued its journey to Southeast Asia via Aden and the Indian subcontinent.

Ruth and her parents lived near the Shell oil refinery in Miri, Sarawak (later Malaysian Sarawak) which was a region of British Borneo at the time.

Ruth (aged 5) & Ethel in Port Said en route to British Borneo

Ruth & 'Tiny'. Ruth celebrated her 6th birthday on board P&O liner
Corfu en route to British Borneo: 30 Nov 1937.

These were pioneering days for the oil industry in Malaysia. Miri had been founded in 1910 when what is now called the 'first oil well in Malaysia' was drilled there on Canada Hill by Shell. In Miri they enjoyed the expat lifestyle for four years, despite the outbreak of the Second World War in Europe in 1939. As a civilian petroleum engineer, Ronald was in what was known as a Reserved Occupation, which meant his job was too valuable to the war effort for him to be conscripted into the British Armed Forces.

Ruth (aged 7) in fancy dress: Miri, Christmas 1938

There was a lively social club in Miri for Shell employees and their families, which included a restaurant, bar, swimming pool, tennis courts, playing fields and social events for both the adults and their children, including fancy dress parties at

Christmas. Holidays were spent in the British Crown Colony of Singapore, about 750 miles away, where Ethel bought most of her and Ruth's clothes and where Ronald had his tropical suits made.

In May 1941, the war came closer as tensions increased between the USA and Japan. Shell evacuated its British employees and their families, initially to Australia in advance of the Japanese invasion of Borneo seven months later.

Ruth (aged 10) in her PLC Orange school uniform:
Orange, NSW 1941

Ruth and Ethel were billeted with the kindly Frank and Beryl Hubbard at their large sheep farm at *Mount Top*, Euchareena, in the state of New South Wales. Ronald stayed with them for 5 months until, in late 1941, Shell flew him, via the

5

Netherlands East Indies (now Indonesia), British Malaya (now Malaysia), Thailand, Burma (now Myanmar), India, Iraq and Palestine, to its oil refinery in Suez, Egypt. Unfortunately, the war in North Africa, which lasted until May 1943, made it too dangerous for his wife and daughter to join him immediately.

Ruth and her mother spent 20 months with the Hubbards[1], enjoying the novelty of farm life and the vast open landscapes and wildlife of New South Wales. Euchareena was near the country town of Orange, where Frank Hubbard's parents were highly respected members of the community and where Ruth attended the Presbyterian Ladies College. Ruth made friends, celebrated her 10th and 11th birthdays there and always retained fond memories of her time in Australia. Ethel remained in touch with the Hubbards for the rest of her life.

In early 1943 Ruth and Ethel sailed west from Sydney to Durban, on the east coast of the South African state of Natal (now KwaZulu-Natal), crossing the German U-boat-infested Indian Ocean en route.

South Africa was then a British Dominion and although Durban was a very multicultural city and a prime holiday resort in southern Africa, many British settlers had set up home there in the past. Ruth attended a local school in Addington, close to the famous South Beach, beloved of local surfers, while her father, from the far north of the African continent, organised the documentation to enable his family to join him in Suez as soon as it was safe to do so.

---

[1] See the later photos of the Hubbards & Ruth at *Mount Top* in 1970 on p168

Ruth (aged 14) with her parents Ronald and Ethel:
Suez, Egypt 1946

The English School Cairo. Image credit: Mohamed Hamza

Finally, in late 1943 Ruth and Ethel sailed north up the east coast of Africa, first to Mozambique and then on to Suez, where they were reunited with Ronald at last. Once they'd settled into their new family home in Suez, Ruth spent seven happy years at the prestigious English School Cairo in Heliopolis, as a boarder, along with children of other Shell staff and of British residents in Egypt. In the year below hers, a young Omar Sharif, later best known for his film roles in *Lawrence of Arabia* and *Dr Zhivago*, also attended The English School.

Ruth (right) with a school friend in Cairo, Egypt: c. 1947

Ruth was a petite but feisty, popular girl with many friends. An enthusiastic hockey player, dinghy sailor and a powerful swimmer (the only female in the Shell Club swimming team, in fact); she also loved art, music, literature and writing, both essays and letters. She planned to start a degree course at Gray's School of Art in Aberdeen, once her family returned home at the end of her father's contract in Suez, but in the meantime Ruth finally completed her secondary education at The English School at the age of eighteen in 1950.

Ruth (aged 19) in Suez: 1950

Ruth (aged 15): Suez 1947

Ruth (aged 16) and Boxer:
Suez c. 1948

Ruth (aged 15) watching a hockey match and
holding her music books: Heliopolis 1947.

Dickie Bird (aged 23) in the Sinai desert: Egypt 1951

That same year she met a young British army officer called John 'Dickie' Bird, who had recently arrived in the Suez Canal Zone with The Loyal (North Lancashire) Regiment to protect British lives and installations from troubles arising from political tensions in that area. They were introduced to each other by Dickie's brother officer, Canadian John Stone, who had married another Shell daughter, Alyson Ashurst. The four of them frequently spent convivial evenings together at the Shell Club or the French Club in Suez, whenever Dickie and John were off duty.

Then the regiment was moved to a camp at Fayid (now Fayed), some 34 miles north of Suez, and Ruth would spend occasional weekends at the Stones' house there to attend parties with Dickie. Whenever Dickie got a precious weekend off, he would borrow an army motorbike and ride it all the way down to Ruth's home in Suez for the weekend.

Ruth (aged 19) in Suez: 1950

On one memorable evening when Dickie was due to visit Ruth, a military emergency arose shortly after he set off from Fayid. Knowing where Dickie was headed, John Stone rang Ruth's home in an effort to contact him. Ruth explained that he hadn't yet arrived and asked if she could give him a message.

"Yes" said John breathlessly: "There's an emergency on. Just tell him codeword 'Flash'. He'll know what it means" – and he hung up.

Intrigued, Ruth waited on the verandah for the sound of Dickie's motorbike. Eventually he arrived, slightly out of breath and very dusty. Parking the motorbike, he dismounted stiffly and removed his helmet. Ruth leaned over the verandah wall and told him about the urgent phone call.

"What did he say?" asked Dickie, still wiping the dust from his goggles.

"He said codeword 'Flash' and that you'd know what it meant" said Ruth, expecting some sort of explanation.

Instead, Dickie rolled his eyes heavenwards and, heaving a great sigh of resignation, replaced his helmet and goggles, kick-started the motorbike and rode hell for leather all the way back to Fayid. Ruth never did discover what the emergency was about, but she was beginning to realise that army life was obviously never dull.

Ruth and Dickie became engaged in 1951 (see her story *The Proposal*). Just before Ruth and her parents left Suez for good that year, The Loyal Regiment was rushed to Trieste, in north-east Italy, to deal with territorial tensions arising on the border with Yugoslavia (now Slovenia). No sooner had Ruth and her parents returned to Aberdeen than Shell offered Ronald the chance to return to Sarawak in a senior position early in 1952. Ruth and Dickie's wedding plans were hastily brought forward to January 1952 so that Ruth's parents could see their only child safely married before they left for Southeast Asia once more (see the story *The Wedding*). At the time of their marriage, Ruth was 20 and Dickie was 24 years old.

Ruth and Dickie went on to raise three daughters, Leslie, Anne and Stephanie, and to enjoy 56 years of peripatetic married life all over the world. Ruth, ever the individual, always spelt his nickname 'Dickey', despite his preferred spelling of 'Dickie'. Since these stories are as she wrote them, her spelling has been left intact.

Anne and Leslie (wearing dresses made by Ruth), Dickie & Ruth (expecting Stephanie): Lancaster, June 1959

In the time-honoured tradition of British army wives, Ruth 'followed the drum' for 27 years, as Dickie, with and without his regiment, was posted to different parts of the world as he rose through the commissioned officer ranks. Italy (Trieste), British Malaya (Ipoh), West Germany (Wuppertal), Malta,

Australia (Canberra) and Sudan (Khartoum) alternated with home postings in different parts of England. In those days it was frowned upon for British army officers' wives to have careers of their own, so Ruth abandoned her plans for a degree in fine art and instead raised her daughters, supported Dickie's career and recreated the family home in new places (both in the UK and abroad) roughly every two years for nearly three decades.

Stephanie, Anne and Leslie (wearing reversible wool cloaks made by Ruth), plus Ruth & Dickie: Preston, Easter 1971

She had been a talented dressmaker for years, creating clothes for herself and her daughters on her sewing machine; she also became a qualified swimming instructor in order to assist teachers at her daughters' school swimming lessons; she joined choral societies in Malta, Canberra and Preston; she worked hard on behalf of local charities wherever she lived; and she was a talented hostess and a sparkling addition to any social event. She was a gifted consort to Dickie and he often attributed his success as much to her as to his own efforts.

Dickie, Ruth and the Yugoslav Military Attaché's wife:
Khartoum 1978

As Dickie says in his Foreword, written shortly after her death in 2008, Ruth also wrote hundreds of lengthy, descriptive, drily witty and hugely entertaining letters to friends and family. Using her favourite turquoise-coloured ink, she wrote in her usual lively speaking style, breaking off when interrupted and continuing later, often with a description of whatever had caused the interruption. Some of her letters, particularly those to her daughters at boarding school, were written in diary style, as she grabbed the odd hour in-between a series of engagements to add another fizzing paragraph to her latest epistle. Everyone begged her to start writing professionally but as Dickie's career progressed and her daughters grew up, she rarely had enough time to concentrate on more than letter-writing.

She wrote only two published articles. *Requiem for Lucette* was penned immediately after we learnt that the beautiful schooner we used to sail in Malta had been sunk by killer whales in the Pacific four years later (it was five weeks before the British family who were sailing her around the world were finally, and to world-wide press attention, rescued); her article was published by Yachting World in 1975. And her *Hello Sailor!* article was published by Dickie's regimental magazine, *The Lancashire Lad*, in the 1980s, to celebrate the regiment's new link with the Royal Navy by way of an official affiliation with HMS Active, a Type 21-class frigate which had served in the 1982 Falklands War.

At long last Dickie retired from his army career, took up the job as Regimental Secretary to what had now become The Queen's Lancashire Regiment and Ruth had the chance to enjoy living in their first owned home in North Lancashire. Now that their daughters had flown the nest, Ruth had time to enjoy being a grandmother to her two beloved grandsons, Anthony and John, who grew up locally. She sang in the local choral society and in the village church choir, joined NADFAS (the National association of Decorative and Fine arts Societies), worked for local and military charities and continued to host and attend a wide variety of social events with Dickie.

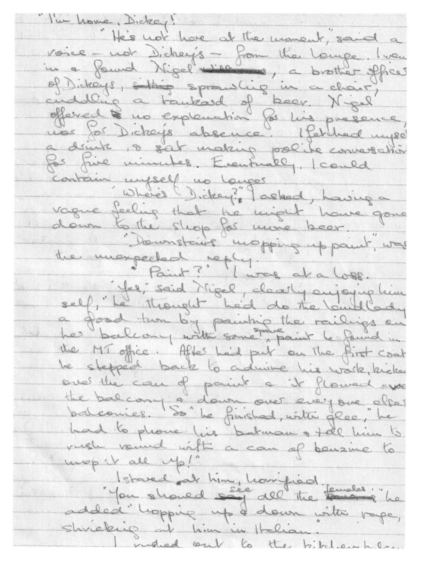

Original story page by Ruth in her favourite turquoise-coloured ink.

Ruth and Dickie at a mayoral banquet: Preston 1979

They enjoyed holidays all over Europe, visiting new places and revisiting old haunts, and they flew further afield to see old friends in Canada and Australia. And all the time Ruth continued to write her wonderful letters to dear friends. She even found the time to compose a few more articles about different events in her adult life, all of which are published here for the first time.

Sadly, and despite having shown the most remarkable courage and stoicism, Ruth succumbed to a long and progressive illness in 2008, a year almost to the day after the death of her middle daughter and mother of her grandsons, Anne. They are buried next to each other in the graveyard of the village where Ruth and Dickie finally chose to settle in 1973. Dickie joined her in 2016.

But Ruth left us this wonderful legacy of her life. We hope you enjoy reading her stories as much as we have enjoyed preparing them for publication.

Leslie Glegg and Stephanie Bruntlett
(Ruth & Dickie's two remaining daughters)
North Lancashire
2020

Foreword by Dickie Bird

Ruth had a way with words and the English language was her love. Many recipients of her letters from faraway corners of the globe will pay testimony to her ability to describe events and people, and to enlighten and amuse all with no hint of hurtful gossip. But this was always on a one-to-one basis in her letters to friends and loved ones and never intended for wider publication.

For years, daughters Leslie, Anne and Stephanie, along with others, tried hard to persuade Ruth to share her adventures. She did write one article about a family sailing adventure which was illustrated and published by Yachting World magazine in 1975, and another funny story for my regimental magazine, The Lancashire Lad, in the 1980s, but she could not at that time be tempted to write more.

Fortunately, the girls and I were eventually able to coax Ruth into some sort of action, albeit reluctantly, for she was convinced that she really had little to say, such was her modesty. Sadly, she managed to pen only a few tales before debilitating illness undermined her energy and ambition to write more.

But we want to share those memories she has revisited with her pen. We hope the reader will enjoy the only too brief records of scenes from the life of one 'camp follower' who followed me, the Regiment and the Flag to the four corners of the earth between 1951 and 1978.

Dickie Bird
Bilsborrow, Lancashire
May 2008

The Proposal - Suez 1951

"You don't want to marry into the army", said Dickey. "It's an awful life for a woman, having to drag around all over the world with kids, and so on."

I was startled, to say the least. I'd never mentioned marrying into the army; moreover, the "dragging all over the world" bit seemed a bit ridiculous to one who'd done it all her life. I said as much, in some indignation: my father was a petroleum oil engineer, and my mother and I had followed the oil-track, so to speak, ever since I could remember. I got my point over and paused for breath.

"That's all right then", said my soldier-suitor, with some satisfaction.

When he'd gone back to camp, thirty miles away in Fayid, I started to wonder what he'd meant. Could it have been a proposal? We'd been going out together for six months – was the time ripe? *I* didn't know. I decided I would have to enquire tactfully next time he came down to Suez - my home.

He arrived the following weekend and, sitting together watching the evening convoy swishing gracefully into the canal under a spectacularly star-studded sky, I decided the moment was ripe for confidences, if any.

"What were you talking about last week?" I asked abruptly.

"Huh?" mumbled Dickey, coming out of a daze.

No luck; I tried again.

"Did our conversation have any deeper significance?" I enquired delicately.

"What *are* you talking about?" said Dickie, with typical male impatience.

I lost my temper.

"Last week", I said, slowly and distinctly, "you told me not to marry into the army. Who said I was going to?"

"Well... aren't you going to marry me?" he asked in surprise. After a pause I said, "Have you asked me?"

"Yes!"

"No you didn't!"

"Yes I did!"

"Well, ask me again – properly!"

He sighed wearily. "Will you marry me?"

Ruth and Dickie after announcing their engagement beside the Shell Club pool: Suez, 1951

The Wedding - Norfolk 1952

And so, several months and many miles later, we were married in England. In Norfolk, to be exact. It had to be Norfolk, because that was as near the centre of Britain as we could manage. My parents and relatives were in Aberdeen, and Dickey's parents and relatives were in Surrey. To have chosen either place would have caused considerable upheaval to one or the other of our respective families. Fortunately, Dickey had a sister living in a tiny village in Norfolk[2]. Accordingly, Dickey and I arrived at her home and informed her that we had chosen her home and village as our base for matrimonial operations.

To our surprise, she showed considerable reluctance to accept the honour. She seemed convinced that the blame for

---

[2] Viv (a nurse) and Peter West (a wartime RAF fighter pilot) lived at Eel Pie House, near Stow Bardolph

this plan would fall at her door. I might add that the month was January, and a particularly cold one at that. The roads were icy and treacherous; no-one, she said, would care to travel at that time of the year, and our marriage would be regarded uncomfortably from all quarters. She was quite right. My mother, when we phoned her, burst into loud sobs. Dickey's mother said "Well really, I do think you might have considered the inconvenience". We brushed all this aside. Dickey had two weeks' leave from Trieste[3], and only a week remained. My parents were due to leave for Borneo. It was now or never.

Accompanied by Dickey's sister and brother-in-law, we bearded the local registrar in his den.

"We want to get married in a hurry" Dickey said.

The registrar peered through his glasses at my fashionably loose coat[4], and then disapprovingly at Dickey. Then he caught sight of Vivienne and Peter, our escort.

"You want to get married in a hurry too?" he snapped.

Vivienne gave a startled giggle.

"Oh no" she said "We're married!"

Aware that there was a deeper significance in this conversation, but not sure just what it was, I kept quiet. The registrar, on hearing the details, said he couldn't do it.

---

[3] The Loyal Regiment was now part of an Anglo-American peacekeeping force, sent to the Free Territory of Trieste to diffuse tensions between Italy and Yugoslavia over territorial disputes in the aftermath of World War II

[4] The Swing coat was hugely fashionable in the 1950s

"Not enough notice" he said, and bent over his desk once more. Thus dismissed, we filed out of the door, somewhat dashed.

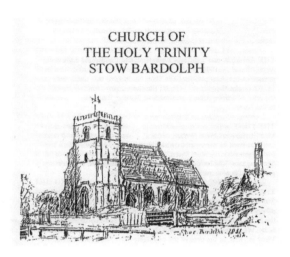

CHURCH OF
THE HOLY TRINITY
STOW BARDOLPH

Ruth & Dickie married in Stow Bardolph Church on 26 January 1952

There was a short consultation, and then we tried the vicar.

"Certainly I can do it" said he "in church, too, with the organ; but as you're under twenty-one you'll have to have written permission from your father" he added to me.

"Why?" I cried, indignant. "I'm over sixteen, and under Scottish law[5] I don't need my parents' consent!"

"Ah" said he, gently "but you're in England now!" Thus it was that my wedding day dawned with Dickey and me breathing heavily on the frosty window-pane, watching for the postman who, we hoped, would bear to us, by means of

---

[5] Unlike Scottish law, in 1952 English law dictated that one had to be over 21 to marry without parental consent

Express post, my father's consent in writing.

When he arrived, skidding along the icy road and brushing the snow off his bag, he was almost engulfed in the excitement. But he had it. Dickey and Peter, his brother-in-law, leapt into the car with our precious document and departed in a whirl of snow for Ely, some miles distant, there to hand our evidence to the bishop, and get *his* written consent. The wedding was timed for 3pm, and by midday Vivienne and I were frantic. The roads were frozen hard, and we expected to receive news of a ghastly crash, but they returned at last, flourishing an impressive-looking paper affixed with a large red seal.

We all bundled into the car again and went to the local pub for lunch. Here, the landlord produced some stone bottles of English mead. It was delicious stuff, and groom and best man

Peter & Dickie arrive at the church from the pub: Norfolk, 1952

partook heavily of this unusual beverage. However, they weren't quite quick enough, as my parents arrived before the bottle was empty, and while Dickey was carefully dividing out the mead, *his* family arrived, cold and indignant: they had driven up, and the roads had given them several nasty moments, and they had been rerouted twice. Dickey reluctantly divided the mead again, and we left in a jollier frame of mind for the wedding, Dickey and Peter going on ahead, leaving deep and uneven tracks in the snow.

The ceremony, surprisingly enough, went without a hitch, and we walked solemnly down the aisle to find, at the door, a pair of photographers. We stood with fixed smiles for some minutes, while the family crowded behind, vainly waving bags of confetti. They were sternly rebuked by the photographers and were sent back into the gloom of the church, still clutching their confetti, for yet another ten minutes. By this time, my smile had become fixed and Dickey's had gone. The family surged out and threw confetti over us, photographers and themselves, and then produced their own cameras. The result was that half the wedding photographs showed groups of the family standing behind us photographing each other, notably my two sisters-in-law, who stood together, smiling toothily, waiting for their photograph to be taken. Alas, at the critical moment, their smiles changed to expressions of chagrin, for my brother-in-law thrust his beaming face between them and, in their opinion, ruined the effect.

Ruth & Dickie's wedding: Norfolk, 26th January 1952

Peter photobombs Dickie's sisters Joan & Viv:
Norfolk, 26 January 1952

And so we all went back to the house from whence we had departed, and were demurely sipping tea when my father said "Tea? Where's the champagne?" Peter produced three bottles, and they were emptied with appreciation.

"No more?" cried my father. "Let *me* look!"
And he finally unearthed three more, which Peter had been saving for another important occasion. Peter watched glumly while these were emptied, and all his brandy, and whisky, and gin.

When the party started on beer round about 9pm, and nobody showed any signs of going home, Dickey and I slipped out and drove round to the local. It was, not surprisingly, empty, as nearly everyone was with our family, happily drinking. We explained to the landlord that we had come out "for some peace and quiet".

At closing time we dawdled back again: the party was still going. We had to slip in the back way and creep quietly upstairs.

Cutting the wedding cake with Dickie's military sword. Peter West brandishing the shotgun on right! Norfolk, 26 January 1952

The Journey - Europe 1952

Dickey procured another fortnight's leave for our honeymoon, then went back to Trieste, leaving me with his sister. I was surprised and woebegone: this was my first taste of army life - it had never occurred to me that I wouldn't accompany my husband. It was explained to me that the army was not, as yet, responsible for me, because Dickey was under twenty-five, and I was officially (to the army, that is) an illegal wife. Soon after Dickey left for Europe, my parents sailed for Borneo. I decided my rôle would henceforth be 'suffering bravely borne', and crept round my sister-in-law's house like the chief mourner at a funeral.

Dickie & Ruth (with Snooper) at Eel Pie House post-wedding:
Norfolk, January 1952

Ruth & Dickie on Pitch Hill: Surrey, February 1952

Eventually, things got under way, and I got a letter from the
War Office stating that I could have a berth on the

MEDLOC[6] train from Hook of Holland to Villach, Austria, where I would be put on a bus which would take me through the Italian Alps to Trieste; I had merely to provide my own transport to the Hook. And, said the letter, would I please acknowledge? Then began a lengthy and involved correspondence about baggage, passports, money and so on, ad infinitum. I parted apprehensively with my passport and prayed that it would be returned in time, got my inoculations up to date, booked a passage on the Channel run to the Hook and arranged for my heavy baggage to follow by sea. Having got everything tied up to my satisfaction, I treated myself to a new hat!

Departure day dawned, and I duly arrived at Harwich via Liverpool Street. Being a great believer in travelling light, I had only one cabin trunk and a small suitcase with me. The trunk was taken twenty-five yards from platform to Customs shed by an enormous porter.

"Thank you so much" I said, smiling brightly.

He looked at me very hard, and eventually held out his hand.

"I won't be seeing you again" he said.

I was surprised and touched: what a charming gesture, I thought, he wants to shake hands. Fortunately the truth dawned in time to avert an embarrassing scene, and I hastily handed over the last of my small change.

On boarding the ship I was shown to my cabin, still muttering to myself about money-grubbing Sassenachs. The

---

[6] **Med**iterranean **L**ines **O**f **C**ommunication train

cabin was small and neat, with two berths. I took the top - I always suffer from claustrophobia in lower berths. My travelling companion arrived and turned out to be an elderly and very shy Dutch lady, who spoke very little English. The cabin being small and the lady large, it soon became evident that, in order to avoid considerable embarrassment and confusion, one of us would have to leave. I took myself up to the deck to wait, shivering, until a suitable time had elapsed to allow my companion to get into her bunk. An hour passed and I returned. The lady, fortunately, was in bed and either asleep or feigning sleep. The cabin was in darkness and I had omitted to unpack my pyjamas. I didn't like to put the light on, so groped around in the dark, turning the contents of my suitcase into a turmoil. As a small pile began to grow around my feet, I was beginning to wonder whether I'd left them behind or packed them in my cabin trunk when a voice said "So easy to see with light!" I put the light on, found my pyjamas and eventually crawled into my bunk, feeling a trifle foolish.

When I awoke next morning, my companion had gone and we were at the Hook. I got myself and baggage on shore in due course and found that I was practically the last to go through Customs - indeed, apart from myself and the Customs officers, the shed was empty. To my horror, no-one appeared to speak English, but they passed me through and I was immediately lost in a maze of halls. I found my way to a restaurant in the building and sat down, feeling lost and aggrieved. I hadn't a notion where to go, nor whom to ask for, nor what to do about my baggage, and for a while I was overcome by blind panic. Eventually reason prevailed, and I asked the waitress about the MEDLOC train. She seemed to catch on to the MEDLOC part, led me to a doorway and pointed across some open ground and railway tracks to a large ugly shed bearing a sign: MEDLOC - Families. Thanking her, I made my way nonchalantly over the rough ground, feeling most conspicuous.

Hook of Holland customs hall: 1950. Image credit: "Hook of Holland: Gateway of the Continent" by Arjan den Boer

There was a large Military Policeman in the doorway, who asked for "Documents please, madam". I handed them over guiltily and wondered why he wanted them. To my unutterable relief he seemed to know all about them, and where to direct me, and what to do about my luggage.

"Don't worry, madam, it'll be on the platform".

He sent me along a corridor and I found a large hall filled with families. I made haste to seat myself among the comforting throng, and happily awaited further developments. Everything was now out of my hands: the army had Taken Over, and I had no more worries.

A small party of WRAC[7] and Welfare officers made their way among the groups, checking and advising. When they reached me, I blandly handed over my papers.

"Oh no, madam" said one, "this is the Other Ranks[8] lounge. You should be in the lounge further along the corridor".

Self-consciously, I collected my things and went out into the corridor. I found the lounge next-door: it was smaller, with fewer families. They all stopped talking and gazed at me with open interest. I made my way to a corner and tried to withdraw as much as possible into a large chair. Conversation was resumed and time dragged by. I glanced up to see a small collection of sergeants making their way round the lounge, inevitably checking documents. Wearily I got mine ready. One of the sergeants glanced at them and said in a penetrating voice "You're in the wrong lounge, madam. This is the WO's[9] and Sergeants' lounge. You should be next door". As before, conversation lapsed while I made my way from the room.

---

[7] Women's Royal Army Corps
[8] The British Army comprises 3 groups: Officers, Non-Commissioned Officers & Other Ranks
[9] Warrant Officers

Attempting to carry it off with an air, I tripped over a small suitcase and fled from the room, overcome with embarrassment.

I hesitated long outside the door of the Officers' lounge which, I noticed, bore a large sign to that effect. A thought struck me. I glanced back along the corridor at the other two lounges. They both bore large notices announcing their business. I felt my face go hot (I never was a notice-reader) and despairingly pushed open the door of the Officers' lounge, heartily consigning the army to an untimely end. The Officers' lounge was vast, with an enormous bar. It was completely empty. I stepped outside and glanced at the sign again. The document-checking sergeants came along the corridor, talking among themselves. Catching sight of me, one of them stopped.

"That's right, madam" he said encouragingly. "In there".
Obediently I stepped inside and the door closed. After half-an-hour two officers came in. They stared at me seated, like a pea on a drum, in solitary splendour, then moved over to the bar and called loudly. A soldier emerged from a door behind the bar and they all started to talk penetratingly together, ignoring me completely. An hour passed. I was in some alarm lest I had been completely forgotten and was wondering what to do about it when an officer with a red arm-band entered and crossed over to me.

"MEDLOC?" he asked.
I nodded, praying that he hadn't come to apologise for having

overlooked me. He hadn't.

As we went out to the platform - myself trotting breathlessly behind - I remembered my baggage.

"On the platform" said my guide serenely, not turning his head.

So it was, under some thirty other cases, trunks and zipper-bags.

"Just sort it out with the porter, would you?" drawled the red-banded deity, already some yards down the platform.

I spotted an aged creature in a grey jacket and cap.

"Are you a porter?" I asked nervously. With so many uniforms around, it was as well to make sure.

"Ja, ja, ja" he returned, jerking his head vigorously up and down, almost dislodging his cap from his grey head.

I hesitantly indicated my baggage. On closer inspection, he certainly looked small and wizened. However, he attacked the pile with vigour, unearthed my trunk and somehow contrived to get it on the train. He then inspected my ticket, showed me to my carriage and whipped out his hand. This I had not foreseen. I was vaguely under the impression that the porters would all be soldiers, and that I would not be required to tip. Despairingly I recalled giving the last of my change to the porter at Harwich. I hunted through my pockets and handbag, without hope. The porter's gaze sharpened; he still held his hand out and looked very suspicious. I had visions of him leaping down the platform and whipping my trunk off the train, just as we moved off.

I took out one of my BBAFs[10] and handed it over, saying earnestly "It's all I've got". He turned it over in some doubt (or was he only piling on the agony?) and eventually accepted it. I withdrew to my compartment feeling distinctly warm about the face and neck.

My compartment was upholstered in dark green and boasted three bunks, one on top of the other. I hoped that I would not be sharing for, although I have a preference for top bunks, this one looked a very long way up. A steward looked in and I asked (in a gabble of words, since everyone I had so far met seemed to rush off before I completed my questions) "What time's the train leaving and am I sharing?". He was vague about the time but said no, I wasn't sharing and lunch was being served in fifteen minutes. It seemed a long day. We soon passed the tulip-fields, and the countryside was flat and monotonous. I was impatient to get to Trieste and see Dickey. The train-noises hummed in my head, and the only distractions were the odd people who kept popping their heads around my door - stewards announcing meals or snacks, officers relieving me of my passport, keys and documents (this last alarmed me considerably, for my father had constantly dinned it into my ears: "Never part with your passport or keys!" Obviously the army didn't trust anyone to look after their own keys and passports) and Customs officials at every other stop - or so it seemed.

---

[10] British Banknotes of the Armed Forces

At some stage in the journey a steward appeared like a genie, announcing "Getting into Cologne, madam". I looked out with interest, for I'd heard that it had been very badly bombed during World War Two and, as yet, having lived abroad, I had seen no large-scale damage. I was appalled to see that whole areas were completely razed to the ground.

Cologne cathedral surrounded by the war-damaged city.
Image credit: David Foster

It seemed a miracle that the twin towers of the cathedral still stood, apparently untouched. As the train moved past the ruins, I wondered what it was like to be bombed, and spent the rest of the evening absorbed in some very sober thoughts. Next morning we click-clacked along beside the Rhine, past steep cliffs and vineyards and craggy, fairytale castles, whilst tugs and barges bustled up and down the brown water.

More Customs officers and we were in Austria and, soon after lunch, we reached the end of our train-journey, Villach. I left the train with relief, but the click-clack still dinned in my ears.

A moving view of Germany from the MEDLOC train to Villach: Austria, 1952

We were shepherded outside the station, myself still desperately enquiring about my baggage. I felt I should never get used to the army's unconcern about baggage: ever since I had once left a suitcase at Southampton, I had felt it necessary to watch my trunks and cases assiduously. The Powers-that-Be, however, considered that wives couldn't be trusted with their baggage. Later, when I had small children of my own to travel with, I had cause to bless this attitude of mind and wonder if, perhaps, the Powers-that-Be showed more foresight than I had first given them credit for. Out in the square stood two coaches, both with trailers. I was intrigued by these last - whoever heard of buses with trailers? I certainly hadn't. I wondered over their safety and was relieved to find that I was riding in the first bus. An Artillery officer and his family arranged themselves in front, two more families behind, and a burly REME[11] sergeant next to me. The rest of the buses and trailers were filled with a draft of very new-looking Military Policemen. The baggage - my nightmare - went on top and, after much shouting and laughter we were off, through the town to the mountains.

Villach postcard: Austria 1952

Steep grassy slopes rose on one side, crowned with black pines, while below rushed a clear shallow river, pines crowding along its banks. I stared around with interest, wondering if we were near the Tyrol and hoping to see men in leather shorts

---

[11] Royal Electrical and Mechanical Engineers

46

and green hats with feathers stuck in the hatbands. Surprisingly, once we had left the town, where the people were dressed like people anywhere else, we saw no-one until, not far from the town, we reached the Austro-Italian border, sheltering under sullen grey cliffs. I chafed at the delay and asked my companion how long the trip would be.

"About five hours, I think" said he cheerfully.

I felt pale: five hours, cooped up in this crowded bus, and I suffered from car-sickness! However, the sergeant proved an interesting conversationalist, and the first hour passed pleasantly enough. We pulled into a tiny grey-stoned marketplace, in front of a small inn. An arm-banded officer appeared from the second bus and announced: "This is Tarvisio, where we stop for fifteen minutes. You can get coffee in the albergo here; our next stop will be Udine, on the other side of the mountains".

Incidentally, I had observed this officer, on our embussing at Villach, signing for the buses, which had amused me considerably.

"He's taking them over" the REME sergeant had said. "You have to sign for everything in the army, otherwise things get lost".

I thought of the authorities frantically searching for two buses and about fifty men, lost between Villach and Trieste, and various Quartermasters wondering 'who was to pay?'. The Tarvisio inn was a delightful old building, full of unexpected stairs and grilled windows and huge fireplaces, and with dull glowing murals all over the walls. I gazed at two doors, one inscribed Signori and the other Signore; unable to decide which meant Ladies and which Gentlemen, I decided not to bother, and accepted instead a large cup of foamy coffee from my travelling companion.

First stop in Tarvisio on the coach from Villach to Trieste: Italy, 1952

Several miles later, I had cause to regret my cup of coffee, and waited anxiously for the next stop. It seemed as if the grey soaring walls on either side would never end. In a deep gully to one side of the road ran a river of startling pale green - almost turquoise; its stones were dazzling white.

"I expect" said the sergeant "that there is some mineral in the water which affects its colour".

The road was narrow and winding, with far too many blind corners for comfort. The buses tore along at a terrifying rate, horns blaring a tuneful fanfare, trailers rocking and swaying behind. Once, we passed another bus and trailer going the other way. It was a nerve-racking moment and took my mind off my own worries for a short time. The novelty of our mountain drive soon wore off, however, and my thoughts returned to that fateful cup of coffee.

"How much longer do you think it is?" I asked.

"Oh, about another hour" was the cheerful answer!

At last we reached Udine and turned into the courtyard of another inn. This proved to be a sprawling sort of place and, try as I might, I could not find the ladies' room. At last, desperate, I found a little waitress.

"Where's the ladies' room?" I asked in a low voice.

She giggled and broke into a spate of Italian. I was horrified. Hopefully, I tried French: no luck. We were joined by another waitress: I tried English and French on her, without success. Despairingly I tried Arabic, a long shot that didn't come off. Two more waitresses came over. I gave up hope; the only alternative was mime. I proceeded elaborately to wash my hands in air. They giggled and conferred among themselves. I tried again, and they copied me. We were all madly rubbing our hands when a splutter made me look up. We were being observed, with interested amusement, by the entire draft of Military Policemen. Overcome, I retreated to the bus. It was empty, except for a middle-aged lady with a little boy.

"Ladies' room, dear? Just through that door over there!"

It was dark when we reached Trieste, along a cliff road with the sea shimmering dully far below us, and the lights of the city spread like a sparkling tiara at the end of the bay. The first sound that struck me on stopping was that of countless motor-scooters, streams of them, roaring up and down the road. I was stiff and tired and confused by the noise and darkness, and it was a relief to hand over to Dickey once more.

The Job - Trieste 1952-3

Trieste was delightful; a lovely city, climbing in tiers like a wedding cake, and ringed by green hills. The Adriatic lay at our feet, a clear, sparkling blue, glimmering over shadowy rocks and patrolled by restless schools of fish. It was spring, and the chestnut trees were shaking white blossoms on the sidewalks, wisteria was hanging thickly from the walls, and occasional thunderstorms crashing over the city sent people laughing and shouting for shelter. Here everybody laughed and shouted, and the streets at evening were filled with people, dressed in their best, drifting along, greeting friends, sipping caffè espresso in the numerous *albergos* - a gay, restless, shifting stream. There was a zest for life here which I had never met before: by day the cobbled squares, with their gaily covered stalls, were a kaleidoscope of colour; by night the town scintillated.

Postcard of Piazza Unità, Trieste by night: 1952.
Image credit: Rotalfoto Milano

But our idyll soon came to an end.

"Off to Austria next month" said Dickey cheerfully.

"Austria?" I queried, startled.

"Oh, not you, dear" he said kindly. "Only the men. On manoeuvres, you know".

"How long for?" I felt a momentary coolness towards him. How could he be so cheerful at the thought of leaving me?

"Only a month"

"A *month*?"

This was worse than I had anticipated. And he seemed so pleased - and guilty because he felt he shouldn't be pleased.

"Oh, all right" I said, airily. "I'll pop along and get myself a job".

If I had expected to shatter him, I was wrong. He received my idea with such enthusiasm that I felt quite dashed. Damn it all, now I'd *have* to work! I stalked out of the room in a huff.

Dickie (standing, 3rd right), Ruth (seated, 3rd right)
& their friends: Trieste, 1952

And so I went to work for Military Intelligence which, in Trieste, was combined - American and British. The chief clerk was an American sergeant who hailed from Kentucky and was just the sort of soft-voiced gentleman that I expected Kentuckians to be.

There was also an American corporal - a sophisticated, quick-talking young man whose home town was Cleveland, Ohio - and two British corporals. On my first day at work, I was interrupted by the chief clerk, who wanted to show me his wedding photos. It appeared that he had been married three weeks, and he had invited everyone in the building, British and American, to attend his wedding reception.

"It was quite a party" he enthused. "There's my wife - she's Italian, you know".

I gazed with interest at the photos and noticed that his wife had chosen to be married in a very smart straight white coat. She was lovely, and I said so. The chief clerk was very pleased.

"Odd" I thought "that she should choose a coat to be married in", but I didn't think any more of it, for I had more work on my hands than I had anticipated.

View from Castello di San Giusto towards Trieste harbour: 1952.

My British bosses kept paperwork to a minimum and went about their work in a leisurely kind of way, but my American bosses were a different matter. True to the association in my mind of American businessmen, these Americans kept up a constant high-pressure of work, and filed papers about everything. We were literally snowed under with paperwork, and I began missing lunch-hours to keep up with it.

One morning, when I had been there two months, I was surprised to find the chief clerk's desk empty. This was quite an occasion, for he was usually at his desk an hour before I arrived in the morning.

"Where is he?" I asked Dent, our Cleveland representative. Dent shifted his gum to the other cheek and said, laconically "Gone to buy some cigars".

"Huh?" I asked, speechless.

"Yeah" said Dent, leaning back in his chair and watching me with his eyes half-closed. "He wants to hand 'em out. He's a father. Son born this mornin'".

I laughed. "Oh, you're fooling" I said, taking the cover off my typewriter.

"Why should I be?" His voice was sharp.

I looked up in surprise. He was bent forward, watching me intently. I opened my mouth to say "Because he's only been married two months", and then I realised that that was exactly what he was waiting for me to say, so he could mock me for being such a little innocent. And suddenly I remembered the wedding pictures, and the bride in her straight white coat. I shut my mouth and hesitated, and then said "Why should you be? Because you usually are, of course!" And started typing furiously, drowning whatever he had been going to say. When an hour had passed, and the chief clerk had danced through the office, thrusting cigars at everybody and singing "It's a boy! It's a boy!" I was very glad that I hadn't let myself fall into Dent's trap. And I made a note to watch these quiet Kentucky

US army in Trieste: 1952.
Image credit: US Army's Together We Served website

gentlemen in future!

Of our two British corporals, one was a quiet individual who kept to himself, and was usually hidden in the filing-room. The other was a rather superior young man, well-spoken, who knew all the regulations backwards. He had occasional digs about officers, but I ignored them, believing that he was trying to provoke me into an argument. However, one day I was taken unawares when he suddenly burst out:

"You know, officers are an idle bunch! I mean, they do damn all! *We* do all the work! Just tell me what an officer does!"

Never having been an officer, I couldn't tell him, and said so. I was about to add that, furthermore, I didn't want to hear any more 'bolshie' talk when, emboldened by my temporary defeat, he continued:

"Let's face it, just how much work does your husband do? Not enough to keep him occupied, admit it!"

I was speechless. Appalled by his rudeness, brashness and lack of taste, I could find nothing to say. And my last month with my husband (then MTO[12]) had been spent watching him work out the movement to Austria (and various other details unintelligible to me) every evening. The injustice brought so many words to my tongue that I choked on them. Dent, who had been watching in interested silence, turned to Corporal Morris.

"Beat it" he said calmly.

Morris beat it. For the rest of my stay with the MI, Morris and I took pains to avoid one another.

---

[12] Mechanical Transport Officer

Piazza Unità

Castello di San Giusto

Trieste

DIY - Trieste 1953

Eventually Dickey returned from Austria, and my need for an occupation had gone. However, I couldn't find a valid reason for deserting my post, and remained with the MI, feeling most dissatisfied with my lot - I much preferred to be a housewife, wandering round the gay, noisy markets, to flogging in an office. Dickey was quite satisfied with our arrangements until the day of our regimental holiday dawned: naturally, it was no holiday for the MI section, and so Dickey stayed in bed while I went off to work. Needless to say, I felt more dissatisfied with my labours than ever.

It seemed a very long day, hot and irritating; my fingers slipped off the typewriter keys as the sweat dripped off my hands; I could feel my scalp prickling with perspiration. I felt tired and limp as I rode up in the lift to our flat on the fourth floor. The front door was open. I felt my spirits rising - how kind of him, I thought, to leave the door open in such a welcoming way. He's probably getting me a cold drink. I walked into the hall and called "I'm home, Dickey!"

View from Ruth & Dickie's flat towards hills overlooking Trieste: 1952

"He's not here at the moment", said a voice - not Dickey's - from the lounge. I went in and found Nigel, a brother officer of Dickey's, sprawling in a chair, cuddling a tankard of beer. Nigel offered no explanation for his presence, nor for Dickey's absence. I fetched myself a drink and sat making polite conversation for five minutes. Eventually I could contain myself no longer.

"Where's Dickey?" I asked, having a vague feeling that he might have gone down to the shop for more beer.

"Downstairs, mopping up paint" was the unexpected reply.

"Paint?" I was at a loss.

"Yes," said Nigel, clearly enjoying himself, "he thought he'd do the landlady a good turn by painting the railings on her balcony with some spare paint he found in the MT office. After he'd put on the first coat, he stepped back to admire his work, kicked over the can of paint and it flowed over the balcony and down over everyone else's balconies. So," he finished with glee, "he had to phone his batman[13] and tell him to rush round with a can of benzene to mop it all up!"

I stared at him, horrified.

"You should see all the females," he added, "hopping up and down with rage, shrieking at him in Italian."

I rushed out to the kitchen balcony: sure enough, it was a glistening dark green - but so was the floor and so, on inspection, was the sun blind immediately below. Voices floated up from below: "Oh, tutti i fiori[14], tutti i fiori!" in a soaring soprano; and a breathless baritone, "They'll be quite all right when I've got the paint off, Signora!"

---

[13] An army officer's personal soldier-servant
[14] It means "All the flowers!" in Italian

Dickie & Nigel at 'The Boot' (note the shape of the beer glasses!):
Trieste, 1952

Flat kitchen & balcony with railings on extreme left: Trieste, 1952

Eventually a weary and paint-spattered Dickey arrived, followed by a small soldier carrying a large can and grinning in a highly insubordinate manner.

Dickey explained that he had been:

    a) pacifying the lady immediately below for splashing paint on her wooden sun-blind, and assuring her that the only answer was to paint it green all over, as it would be much cooler that way

    b) sponging paint off the geraniums belonging to the lady on the second floor (which accounted for the cries of "tutti i fiori!")

    c) offering to replace the articles of clothing belonging to the lady on the first floor, whose washing had been 'painted'

    d) promising to replace the sun canopy belonging to the gentleman (who wasn't being very gentle) on the ground floor.

For some time after this mishap, Dickey and I avoided our neighbours, while having 3rd Floor's blind painted, buying 2nd Floor new geraniums and purchasing a new canopy for Ground Floor. This last proved so expensive that we almost fell on 1st Floor's neck in gratitude when she said she'd managed to salvage her clothing. And for the rest of our stay there, people used to keep a wary eye on Dickey whenever he came out on the balcony, rolling up their blinds and hastily taking in their washing and flowers.

Beyond the Pale - Malta 1965-8

"I'll *never* race with you again!" I told my husband. And I never have. Mind you, I haven't been invited. The scene was the Garrison Sailing Club, Malta, at the top of Marsamxett Creek, a sunny, blowy Saturday afternoon, and we had just arrived to do some work on the army Folkboat. Everyone was rushing around, kitting up for a dinghy race, and Dickey was stirred by the excitement and bustle.

"Let's race too", he said. But the dinghies were all taken. "Never mind, I'll find two more bodies and we'll race in the Folkboat."

"In a dinghy race?" I asked, doubtfully.

"Just for fun."

"But we'll get in the way."

"Then *everybody* will have fun!" he said, rushing off. He was soon back. "Everyone's booked", he said "we'll take it out ourselves". I protested - over the years my spouse's enthusiastic notions have turned me into an automatic protester. However, I helped rig the Folkboat and cast off, and we jockeyed around the start line, testing the wind and timing ourselves to reach the line as the gun went off.

The race was a broad reach up the harbour, round the buoy

Folkboat race, off Malta: 1967-68

and beating home. We duly crossed the start line in good order, and I had settled down for a peaceful reach when Dickey said, "I think I'll break out the spinnaker."

"What for? We're not going far. We can't even be counted in the result", I gabbled.

"It's good practice."

"Who", I asked fearfully, "is going to handle the spinnaker?"

"I am", he said, "Here, take this." And he thrust the tiller and main sheet into my hand.

"I can't hold everything!" I wailed.

"Of course you can! We're reaching[15], aren't we? And when we round the buoy I'll drop the spinnaker and take over again."

It seemed simple. I could find no loopholes. The wind wasn't all that strong, and with the spinnaker up we were certainly whizzing along. Unfortunately, it impeded my view. I considered mentioning this, but cowardice prevailed and I sat mute. Suddenly the spinnaker belled upwards, and in the curve beneath I saw the buoy. Completely forgetting that I wasn't in a dinghy, and that I had a lot more sail and weight than usual, I bawled "Lee-oh!" and pushed the tiller hard over. We skidded around the buoy like a body on a banana skin. Dickey madly started gathering handfuls of spinnaker, which eddied, swelled and fell to one side, revealing a small fleet of Maltese gentlemen dead ahead, each one in a small boat from which lines dangled, disappearing into the water; they were peacefully smoking and chatting when we burst into their conversation. I could hear screams, shouts, curses - as I tore through them I saw, briefly, arms hauling in lines, reaching for oars, fists waving, the splash as someone dived into the sea. Horrified, momentarily distracted, I kept the tiller over a fraction too long and we continued to round the buoy. The spinnaker was plucked from Dickey's scrabbling fingers, flung itself aloft and

---

[15] Nautical term meaning the wind is coming from the side

then fell, completely enveloping him. Past his heaving, fumbling form I saw, yet again, the Maltese fishermen. Our reappearance froze them into immobility. Shocked, they gaped at me, eyes and mouths wide. Their companion who had flung himself overboard was in the act of re-boarding his small craft, but now started swimming madly towards the shore. Miraculously, I had hit nothing on my first circuit and the luck was still with me. As I tried to grab the jib sheet without losing the main or releasing the tiller, I could hear roars of broken Anglo-Saxon fading behind me.

My attention was now on the fast approaching dinghies.

Fisherman in Marsamxett Harbour: Malta, 1966

Dickey's head appeared, the muffled cries he had been giving now clarified - indeed, clarioned - and he continued to struggle blasphemously with the spinnaker, some of which seemed to be tied round his ankles. We were on a starboard tack, heading for the Lazaretto wall. I could see two nuns sitting upon it, sleeves rolled up, skirts hoisted, fishing. Their faces were little dots under their coifs.

"Shut up!" I roared. "The nuns will hear you!"

"Nuns? What - nuns?"

"Ahead!"

Their faces had grown larger, watching us. Now I could discern faint alarm. The wall seemed larger, too. I glanced over the side: through the clear water, the rocks seemed inches below the surface.

"For God's sake," I shrieked, "come and help me!"

The nuns half rose from their perch, consternation and indecision clearly visible now. Trailing curtains of spinnaker, Dickey fell into the cockpit and reached for the jib-sheets.

"Put her over", he snapped. We made a little wash as we went about, spattering droplets at the nuns' feet, then tacked in dignified silence back down the creek, the dinghies now preceding us like darting butterflies. Still in complete silence we stowed everything away, made fast and rowed ashore.

"I'll *never* race with you again!" I said.

Flight from Malta - Malta 1968

I can recall, in my time as a young army wife with baby and small children, the chaos of regimental moves - the families' part, that is. There were various wild-eyed men known as Movements Officers who kept leaping into doors marked 'Private' or 'Gents' and shrieking "My sergeant will deal with that!" To their credit, the sergeants always did, and with monumental calm. Were they made of sterner stuff, more used to life's hurly-burly? Probably the answer is that they knew they could always pass it back to Higher Authority and let him carry the can. But I never realised the stress they were under until I took over the rôle for one family.

The lady was an old school friend and had also been a neighbour in those days. She married into another regiment, and we occasionally coincided on tours of duty. This tour was in Malta and we were all delighted. Eventually their time came to an end and they were posted back to the UK. Since it was February, and their next quarter was not yet ready for them, her husband suggested that she might stay with us for five weeks before joining him in England.

The baby and Stephanie on the balcony:
Malta, spring 1968.

No problem, because two of my children were away at school and my eight-year old would be glad of the company of their eight-year old and the one-year old baby. So we settled down to a very pleasant five weeks, with only one slight flaw: the lady was unpunctual. Well, she always had been and always would be and it didn't worry me overmuch, it just maddened my mate.

The time drew near for their departure, which was booked for a 10am arrival at RAF Luqa and a noon take-off. There were two aircraft passing through en route to Lyneham from Libya, bringing the Paras back from an exercise. They would be very full, but seats had been left for official postings. My husband was due to sail to Sicily that morning, but I could take him to the Sailing Club at 8.30am and be back in time to collect the others and drive them to the airport. A Land Rover was coming to collect the baggage.

As the time neared, a creeping unease began to spread

BEA Malta Service Vickers Viscount at Luqa Airport: Malta, 1967

through me. Why was there no sign of packing?

"Can you get it all in?" I asked nervously, peeping into her room with heaps of clothes, baby bedding, nappies and shoes all over the floor. She assured me that there was no problem. Three days to go and I said, "Should we buy another suitcase?"

"No, no," she said brightly, "it'll all go in, and I'll need the nappies in a carrier bag anyway, and his feed and so on."
I lay wide-awake in bed that night and thought back to our schooldays in Egypt. Her mother did all her preparation and packing for school. At the end of term we, her schoolmates, madly did her packing as we were waiting to be collected for departure, while she sat on her bare mattress, weeping and wringing her hands. Surely, after all her years as an army wife, she could pack by now? Her husband had made no mention, not even a warning note. She wasn't a schoolgirl now; I could hardly storm into her room and take over.

Two days to go and her eight-year old went off her food. So did I. I wasn't sleeping so well, either. One day left, and one suitcase had something in it. Later in the day, she'd taken everything out again. She continued cheerful and chatty, while I had become morose and introverted. I watched the day dawn over the sea. There was no activity from her room. I took her a cup of tea. Her floor was heaped as before, her cases empty.

"Why haven't you packed?" I cried. "You've got to be there at 10am and it's 8am now!" "Yes, yes, I'll be ready'"

"Don't fuss", said my husband as we drove to the sailing club. "She's a grown woman now!" At the club he remembered that he had a sail that needed repair. Would I drop it into the sail maker? It wouldn't take long.

It took longer than I anticipated and it was 9.45am before I got back to the house and saw the Land Rover waiting. Leaping out of my car, I saw that the driver was known to me: he had been my husband's batman but their temperaments had clashed. He was looking decidedly temperamental now. Through the open window I could hear loud sobs and the baby screaming.

"Aren't they ready?" I asked.

"No!" he said, briefly.

I ran into the house. Her eight-year old was in the sitting room, huddled in a chair and weeping quietly. She raised a tear-swollen face and said piteously, "I prayed to God last night not to let it happen, but He didn't listen!"

"Yes He did:" I said, "I'm here now, don't you worry."

In the kitchen I found our Maltese maid, cradling the baby and comforting him. Her face was angry. She jerked her head aloft, from whence the booming sound of noisy weeping echoed down the stone stairway. Upstairs was chaos, suitcases half-packed, the lady herself flung on the bed, racked with sobs. I went mad, yanked her upright - and she was a large lady! - and shouted, "Shut up, get up and shove things in anywhere!" Startled, she gulped into silence and obeyed. I worked with frantic haste, into suitcases, sit on lid, snap shut and lock, into soft bags, zip up and lock and, finally, there were no more bags and still too much left. I flew downstairs and rushed out to the driver. Pushing some money into his hand, I said "Drive round to the NAAFI, would you, and buy two expanding suitcases?"

"I'm not a bloody butler'" he snapped.

My pent-up fury boiled over. I've no idea what I said, but he jumped into his vehicle and roared off. Meanwhile I searched for rope. Back he came with cases and we threw the last lot in. The cases popped off their expanders, as I had feared they might, but he and I lashed them round with the rope and then loaded them into the vehicle and off he went.

I had phoned the RAF Family Movements earlier and warned them that their passengers would be somewhat delayed, but would be there by 11am; I hoped that would hold them, for they were notoriously fussy about their passengers being present two hours before departure. Now I turned my attention to the family. The maid had washed, fed and dressed the two children and the lady would have to manage as best she could, but now there was a new problem: hand baggage. She had to take two huge loaves of Maltese bread to her sister-in-law, and they went into a plastic carrier bag. She had to change her shoes during the flight because her feet swelled. Another plastic carrier bag, plus cardigans. She needed make-up: another bag. Nappies, baby feed - we ended up with seven carrier bags. I loaded them in the boot, shoved in the family and set off.

As I stopped outside the door of the Departure area it was 11am exactly. I felt a million years old, but my ordeal was nearly over.

"Go in and report," I said, "I'll bring the bags."

Struggling to hold seven bulky plastic bags and trying to close the boot, I glanced up and beheld her standing at the top of the steps, tears streaming down her face, her little girl beside her and the baby in her arms.

"Oh God," I said, "What now?"

"They've put me off the flight" she said.

Inside my head I could hear myself screaming, "I can't go through all this again!" Adrenalin poured through me and I was furiously angry.

"They can't," I snapped. "You're not indulging[16]. You're a family posting!" and I stormed in to find the Movements Officer. He proved to be a squadron leader not much taller than myself, and I'm 5ft 2ins. He had fierce red hair, a fierce red face and a red nailbrush moustache. Eyeball to eyeball we glared at each other and argued. He said that he wasn't going to argue, they were off the flight. I said that they were here in good time, as I had told Movements they would be, and he couldn't give their place for 'indulging' as they were a bona fide posting. All the while the lady towered over him, weeping quietly on his head, whilst the baby screamed in his ear and the little girl clung to her mother's skirts and howled. Suddenly a hand touched my shoulder and a calm voice said, "Take her into the departure lounge and wait. I'll see to this." It was her husband's successor - he's now a brigadier, and I hope he ends up as a field marshal, because he earned it! In no time at all

---

[16] A discounted flight for off-duty armed forces personnel or their families to any destination on military transport.

everything was sorted out. I always wonder if our driver had made an unwary comment when he delivered the baggage, which had caused the squadron leader to refuse to load it and started the fuss.

However, we sat and waited with the other passengers, who studiously avoided us, including her husband's late boss and his family, who were unfortunately travelling on the same flight.

Luqa Airport passenger lounge: Malta, 1967.

The lady's tears continued to stream down her face while I cuddled the baby and chatted to the little girl. At last they were called to the boarding gate. I waited tensely in the departure lounge, for I couldn't see the aircraft. Would it 'go technical'? After an eternity I heard the engines at full power roar down the runway and fade into the distance. My bones felt as if they had melted. I rose wearily to my feet and turned to pick up my handbag. Beside it was her handbag, containing all her Movements papers, rail warrants, passports and money. I was still staring at it when the RAF Movements corporal came into the room.

"Not gone yet?' he said cheerily. I pointed to the handbag.

"It's hers" I said. He knew instantly who I meant.

"Never mind," he said, "the next load are coming through in half-an-hour. I'll give it to them, she'll get it, don't worry."
I couldn't see how she would get it in time, but I was quite beyond caring. I went home, took some aspirin, shut the curtains and went to bed.

I heard, subsequently, that the second aircraft had been a faster model, had passed the lady's aeroplane and arrived before her. As she came down the aircraft steps at RAF Lyneham, a grinning corporal was standing at the bottom, holding up her handbag. I also heard about the hullabaloo raised during her flight when she discovered it was missing: how the pilot had refused to radio a message about it and she had become so distraught that her husband's late boss had had to take her in hand. The weary, dusty Paras, crammed in uncomfortably with their kit, must have loved it.

Requiem for Lucette - Malta 1968

(This story was originally published in Yachting World magazine in February 1975)

When we heard the news that Lucette had gone down, we were filled with grief and draped her picture with black cloth, subsequently boring our friends with tales of endurance under sail, particularly Lucette's sail. It was some time before we thought of the unenviable sufferings of the Robertson family, who had been her last crew, and of the awesome expanse of Pacific Ocean on which they had been isolated; inevitably, our thoughts returned to our own family trip in Lucette, recalled with nostalgia and laughter.

We were based in Malta, and my husband had been admiring Lucette and found that her owner was willing to lend her to the army for adventure-training.

Dickie (in cap) and crew on Lucette: Malta 1967

There being little else that could be described as adventurous on the island, she was soon in constant demand, sailing to and from Sicily with soldier crews pretty regularly. All the same, I was a little hesitant when my husband suggested hiring her for a week, along with another couple, and taking both families to Sicily during the summer; not because I was unused to sailing, but I do like to sleep on terra firma. However, Dickey's enthusiasm was not to be denied and he and Brian Woods, another sailing soldier, began to plan the expedition, which was to be in July, when all the storms would be over, and our children back from boarding school.

Our crew finally consisted of four adults - self and Dickey, Brian and his very competent wife Bridget, who had been a WRAC officer and proved to be an organising genius and to possess an iron constitution impervious to inclement weather; four teenagers - my two eldest daughters, my nephew, and the son of a friend in England who had never been under sail in his life; four small children - one was mine - and my Siamese cat. Twelve in all, not counting the cat.

We were instructed to arrive at the quayside at half past two, and just before leaving the house I gave the cat some sardines, knowing she would not eat in a strange place. When we got to the quay, we found Brian changing out of wet clothes and Dickey bleeding from a cut on the forehead; they were a little confused and both started talking at once, giggling feebly to show that all was well, and convincing us that both were hysterical. It appeared that the end of the topping lift had been temporarily fastened to the gangplank to keep the latter out of the way, since it was quite easy to step down onto the deck without using it; Brian, carrying two heavy cans of fuel for the engine, decided that it would be unwise to jump down to the deck and absentmindedly stepped onto the gangplank. The topping lift parted, the gangplank collapsed and Brian, with his two cans, vanished through the thick crust of sewage, dead chickens, oil slick and rotting vegetation that the wind had carried into the harbour. When he reappeared he was still valiantly holding his two cans, proving that the buoyancy of the Mediterranean is not far below that of the Dead Sea. However, since he seemed to be in some discomfort, he was pulled out and advised to disinfect himself and to burn his clothing, and Dickey turned his attention to the topping lift, the block of which had also gone overboard. Corporal Gallia, the boatman and always a willing helper, volunteered to go up the forty-foot mast to attach the new brass block, which was quite large, and Dickey stood below to advise; with the inevitability of a Marx Brothers film, the block fell from Corporal Gallia's grasp and ricocheted off Dickey's forehead into the sea, felling him to the deck. If it had been a more direct blow it would have killed him; indeed, he thought for a fleeting moment that he was among the departed, but he didn't even lose consciousness. When his streaming eyes had refocused, he drove back to the yacht chandler for yet another block and, when we arrived, this was being adjusted by Corporal Gallia who, I noticed, was avoiding my eye.

After we had calmed down I reported that the wind, barely felt at the end of the long harbour, had risen considerably and most unseasonably, and was blowing a gregale (a north-easterly) into our harbour, and then went below with Bridget to load tins of food. We had a large collection of tins, bearing in mind the size and appetites of the crew, and by the time we had them all neatly packed away we were being called to help with the sails.

Ruth (with a friend) at the helm of Lucette: Malta 1968

Lucette was a Staysail schooner, almost fifty years old, nineteen ton and forty-three feet; she had five sails, the largest of which was the genoa, which the less experienced sailors soon came to loathe, as they struggled with its vast size and broke their nails on its unbending folds. As we tacked up the harbour the wind increased until, finally, we burst out into the open sea from behind the mole, caught the full weight of the weather and heeled over at an alarming angle, sailing on one ear, so to speak. The children screamed with half-afraid excitement, the teenagers gasped and hung on, our novice paled and from below there came a resounding crash, accompanied by terrified screams from the cat. Brian and I clambered below with some difficulty to find that the cupboard door had given way under the sudden surge of tins, which were crashing around the deck with the wailing cat underneath. I picked her up and she clung to me, trembling and crying, and with the other hand I held up the cupboard door whilst Brian stuffed the tins behind it. This small task was complicated by the acute angle of the deck, but it was eventually completed and Brian went back on deck leaving me below, bracing my back on the cupboard, my feet in the air against the opposite bunk and holding the cat, who ungratefully disgorged her sardine luncheon onto my shoulder. I wondered gloomily how we would make tea, buffeting along as we were, and then became a little anxious at the thought of tacking into the wind with our very young and inexperienced crew. I was greatly relieved when Brian shortly reappeared to say that, the same thought having occurred to them, it had been decided that we run round to the sheltered side of the island for the night. Accordingly, Lucette gradually became more upright, the motion became gentler, the cat consented to sit on the bunk and the teenagers came clattering below, demanding tea.

The lee side of the island was very pleasant, and we found an empty cove edged with pale gold sun-warmed rocks, where the water looked so inviting that the younger members decided to swim; John, my nephew, proudly produced his new mask and spear gun; I protested about the spear gun since there was nothing to shoot but children, but was assured that it would not be fired when others were in the water, and that they would take turns. All went well for some time and the cat tottered up from the main cabin, encouraged by the laughter; she was clearly appalled by her strange watery surroundings and the children apparently drowning, and rushed below again. Second daughter, Anne, ever adventurous, became too ambitious with the spear gun and fired it into the far distant depths, panicked as the spear disappeared, and dropped the gun, which vanished irretrievably a long way down among rocks. Gloom settled on the party. Bridget came up from the cabin and said the heads were awash; indeed they were, something having gone wrong with the non-return valve, which was returning with such enthusiasm that we looked as if we might go down with all hands, sunk by the loo. It was almost impossible for anyone but a deformed midget to reach the valve, but Brian, head in the loo, body in the galley and legs in the cabin, managed to turn it off. We all applauded his efforts, but he lost a lot of our goodwill when he told us that it would be opened twice a day for half an hour. No problem for males, but there were seven females aboard and three of those were quite small - and we were only at the start of a week on board!

I turned my attention to the cat's toilet arrangements: she had a bowl of torn-up newspaper which she refused to consider, so Dickey suggested that he row her ashore with her lead on, to deter her from seeking refuge once on shore. Anne, recovering from her woe, offered to hold her while Dickey took the oars, and the minute coracle that the Skipper and Mate grandly referred to as 'the dinghy' was lowered over the side. Anne was assisted into position, the cat (enraged by the lead) was handed down, shrieking hysterically, and Dickey, with difficulty, squeezed himself into the stern, which immediately began to sink; we rescued Anne and the cat and Dickey went below to change into dry clothes. The cat went below too, and didn't reappear.

Next morning we set off again, heading across the Malta Channel; the wind had dropped and we were almost becalmed on a heaving, lumpy, residual swell and had to use the engine; the sun was very hot and hazy and it became clear, as we slopped our slow way over the water, that the young were not enjoying themselves; I felt sick myself and Brian, at the helm, felt very off indeed. Bridget and Dickey chatted cheerfully and bustled about in the most aggravating way, planning meals and making coffee. The cat stayed on a bunk with her eyes shut. Brian bravely went below to open the valve for our morning half-hour, while Dickey did something complicated with the sextant and John proudly took the helm. Towards teatime, while Brian was having a nap in the cabin, Dickey (at the helm) suggested that I made some tea; Bridget turned on the Calor gas valve on deck and I waited by the cooker to make sure the gas was through then, turning on the gas tap, I applied the match. Nothing happened, and Bridget checked the valve again: "It's open all right", she was saying, when there was an almighty bang and I was standing in a column of flame. Brian leapt off the bunk, grabbed the aerosol fire extinguisher and put out the flames; I had already turned off the tap and Bridget turned off the valve and I trembled my way up to Dickey, heart thumping and feeling dazed.

"I've been on fire", I said, but he was busy chatting to John and didn't hear, so I said it again.

"Don't be silly", he said impatiently, "go and make the tea!" I must have been shocked because, sheep-like, I returned to the cooker, called Bridget to open the valve and, while Brian watched with bulging-eyed incredulity, I replayed the whole scene. As he extinguished the flames for the second time Brian said, between clenched teeth, "For God's sake, get out of here!" Slightly frizzled and lightly tanned, I tottered back to Dickey and said, "You make the tea, I'll take the helm!" They found that the gas pipe had fractured beneath the cooker and I had been standing, with my lighted match, in neat butane.

Over supper we started to plan the night watches and the teenagers, excited by the importance of such a post and much impressed by the thought of drifting under starry skies over a silent sea, enthusiastically offered their support. Planning the washing up rota was not so well received, however, for the

Skipper and Mate were exempt, Bridget and I were in the galley and the job fell to the four teenagers, who muttered discontentedly; Roddy, the novice, and Anne were booked for washing up on deck after supper, and were instructed to make fast the bucket to the deck before dipping it over the side: their subsequent cries of excitement attracted our attention to the eerie greenish glow of plankton in the water, and the washing up sequence became so prolonged that I had to dry up the dishes myself; as I did so, I became conscious of the damp chill of the night air and went below to don my sweater and anorak, instructing the teenagers to do likewise; eventually, everybody had settled for the night and Dickey and I had the deck to ourselves. The throbbing of ships' engines came clearly over the still water, and every now and then their lights sparkled along the horizon; I was surprised to find the waterway so busy, for it seemed quite empty in the daylight. The night air became damper and the deck glistened wetly: I began to shiver, complaining of the cold. Evidently a summer night on the Mediterranean was not to be as warm as I had expected and my sweater was not nearly thick enough; worse, none of the teenagers had clothing any warmer than mine, since I had planned their equipment. I was very glad when my watch was over and handed my sweater and anorak to my relief with the assurance that they would be needed, and went below to roll up in a blanket. We were roused at dawn by Anne, who was taking her turn on deck and felt that we should all observe daybreak.

With Cape Passaro, the south-eastern tip of Sicily, in view, a land breeze came up, strengthening as we neared the coast, and we sailed along at a smart pace, comfortably heeled over and cutting a crisp bow wave. The children were all perched on the fore hatch, enjoying the motion, chattering and laughing when a helicopter swooped over our heads, the crew staring down at us with great concentration. Gaily, we waved to them but they didn't wave back, just shot off sideways and disappeared over the coastline to our left. Twenty minutes later they were back, slightly lower, staring intently. We stared back, puzzled by their interest.

Roddy King at the helm of Lucette: Malta 1968

When Dickey said they were probably Customs or Coastguard watching for smugglers the teenagers were overjoyed: to come under suspicion was apparently their idea of heaven. I felt most uneasy and terribly guilty and was relieved when they flew off, although I kept a wary eye open for Coastguard cutters bristling with guns.

The wind continued to rise, the sea became rougher, and the teenagers drifted back to the cockpit to get away from the spray. We had been crossing a vast bay, but now the land swept closer as we neared the headland just south of Syracuse, and the motion became uneven, causing us to plunge about a bit; conversation ceased and our younger members became a little tense. When we swept into Syracuse harbour we saw that it was long, large and not at all the haven we had expected, for the wind was funnelling into it, blowing us onto a lee shore. We were approaching the quay (a towering cliff of solid concrete) at such an astonishing speed that we all looked anxiously at the Skipper, hoping that he had some idea of slowing down.

"We'll have the engine", he said, and Brian went below to comply; he reappeared with a cry of "She won't start!"

"Never mind", shouted Dickey, turning Lucette into the wind, "over with the anchor, quick!"

And quick it was. As we swung, stern to the quay, he said, "We'll have to get a line ashore" and turned to me.

"Hurry up, put on your swimsuit. You can take it."

Strong swimmer though I am, I'd never swum in such a boisterous sea, and I resolutely turned my gaze from the sight of waves leaping up the side of the quay and hurried below where I found Bridget, also a strong swimmer and taller than I, already donning her swimsuit, which cheered me considerably. The line, as they knotted it round my waist, felt rough and heavy; cheered on by the teenagers, now impatient for their lunch, I dived overboard, kicked to the surface and struck out. As I swam up a swelling wave the line sank in the trough behind me, dragging me down through the water. I was swallowing a great deal of ocean, the quay was getting no nearer and I began to feel real fear, but Bridget spotted the trouble, took up the slack behind me and together we reached our objective. There was no handhold on the rough side of the quay, and it was fairly high above us; as I rose on the crest of a wave I gripped the top and Bridget held up the line, but my fingers trailed down the side as the wave receded. A small knot of Sicilians watched with great interest as we rose and fell at intervals but made no move to assist us. Eventually, with a Herculean effort, pushed from astern by Bridget, I floundered on to the top, pulled in the line and helped Bridget out, and we made the line fast to a bollard. As we sat, gasping on the edge of the quay, we heard Dickey shouting and saw he was beckoning to us, so we swam back to Lucette, expecting praise and admiration. As they hauled us on board, Dickey said "What about lunch, then?" Later, we found a plastic bag jammed in the water intake pipe, the obvious cause of our engine failure.

Lucette moored stern on in Syracuse: Sicily, 1967

Dickey had been to Syracuse before and showed us around the town, eventually leading us to a pizzeria where we stood in a row along the counter, watching the dough being prepared and choosing our fillings from the selection on view. The pizzas were placed in the brick oven next to a wood fire and we gazed, drooling and sniffing, as they swelled in the heat, cheese bubbling on top; as we ate them, piping hot and straight from the oven, we declared them out of this world! The teenagers were fascinated by Syracuse, the boys watchful for signs of the dreaded Mafia, gazing at the men's hands in case they wore one glove, for they assured me that this was a certain sign. I scoffed at this, pointing out that the night was too warm for gloves, even one glove, and a secret society would hardly be so obvious, but they gave me pitying looks and, ignoring me, scouted ahead in a very furtive manner. When we returned to Lucette, where Bridget was putting her children to bed, we found the cat sitting just inboard of the gangplank, neck elongated shoreward, sniffing with great curiosity, but she declined to go ashore and hastily returned to her bunk. The wind dropped and the night was very pleasant.

Next morning, we had a grand tidy-up and wash-down and the men went along to the sailing club for a shave and a shower. Bridget and I thought we'd like a shower too, for we were very salty after our dip; Bridget went along and I said I'd go later; however, when I went to the club I could find no sign of a ladies' shower and the men in the club stared and sucked their teeth as I passed, which I found so unnerving that I left and never got my shower. This was a great mistake, for I was later to find that the traces of salt still on my skin and hair absorbed the heavy dew at night, making me damp and rather chilly. When I re-joined the company, I found that Leslie (Number One daughter) had accidentally dropped John's knife overboard; she followed this by throwing the bucket into the sea when washing up after lunch and forgetting to make it fast:

it sank from sight and Leslie went below in a huff.

We took them all to the Roman amphitheatre in the afternoon and they forgot their differences.

My involuntary imbibing of the harbour water caused loss of voice, which amused the teenagers very much and they couldn't resist teasing. But it had other drawbacks: I was the only one with a smattering of Italian and, as we needed provisions, Bridget and I went off to the market on the following day, where my hoarse whisper aroused embarrassment, curiosity and a collection of strange home remedies. We had found that the easiest way to feed our brood was to make them open sandwiches for lunch and to have a proper meal at night; accordingly, on our return Bridget and I went below and started our assembly line, passing platefuls up to eager hands, while Dickey and Brian sat chatting and drinking beside us. It occurred to us that the children's consumption had increased considerably, and I stuck my head up to ask why this was so: I found the deck overflowing with Sicilian boys, wolfing our sandwiches for dear life. On asking indignantly for an explanation I was assured by Roddy and Anne that these were their friends, with whom they had struck up an interesting conversation by using classroom French and first year Latin.

"There weren't so many at first," they explained, "but they brought their brothers and cousins."

I doubted very much that these avaricious water-siders were merely friendly and ordered them off, my voice cracking in an infuriated squeak; they were most abusive and, once on shore, they began to throw stones at us. I sent the children below and Dickey and Brian came up and told them to go away; some of them did so, but the remainder jumped into the water and sank the dinghy. Roddy was astonished:

"They seemed so nice", he said.

Tigne (on board Lucette), Missing In Action: Syracuse, 1968

Next morning the cat was missing; she had been sleeping on my daughter's bunk when we settled down for the night, after drawing back from the quay and raising the gangplank; she could have jumped the six feet from the raised end of the gangplank to the shore, but could not have jumped back. With increasing alarm the children called and whistled, but only succeeded in drawing a crowd of interested Sicilians; still speechless, I was unable to call her myself and chafed with frustration. We reported her loss to the police, who were amused, and remained an extra day in case she returned, but Dickey thought she had tried to jump back, missed and drowned, for there was no way of scrambling ashore. We left the next morning, very depressed. As we cleared the headland into a stiff breeze and a boisterous blue sea I took the helm; we could see porpoises skimming just below the crests of the waves alongside us, but their very joy accentuated my own misery and I sat watching the compass and the sea, blinking back tears. If anyone sees a Siamese cat with a knot in her tail in Syracuse, her name is Tigne (pronounced 'teeny') and she's ours.

Towards evening the weather became very rough and we were tacking into a head wind, getting very wet and grumbling over the sail changes; Bridget and I, making supper, missed the warning cry and were suddenly cascaded with plates and tins as we came about, which made us a little indignant. Sitting in the cockpit after sunset I started to shiver, and eventually the shivering became uncontrollable tremors; I felt cold and wet bone-deep. After a while Dickey noticed my ague and sent me below, but I had great difficulty in moving, trembling violently and unable to grasp handholds and, once below, couldn't remove my damp outer clothing. Leslie came to my aid and rolled me up in a blanket, but blanket and bunk felt damp too, and I lay, trembling and worrying and watching the engine-room door swinging open and shut. The teenagers were feeling unwell or damp or tired and soon came below, leaving Brian (who was feeling sick again) at the helm, and Dickey and Bridget coping with the sails, tacking into a rough sea and with no watch to relieve them. The motion was very violent and, sometime in the night, Bridget came down to change out of her wet clothes and laughingly told me how she and Dickey had changed the headsail, with Dickey out on the bowsprit with a lifeline:

"He went under completely, twice," she said cheerfully, "right through a wave."

I was alarmed but she assured me that all was well, though they were rather tired.

"We could do with some hot coffee," she said, "we're very wet and cold."

Consumed with guilt, I slid to the floor and staggered along the tilting deck, angling first one way, then the other; as I passed the heads, we tilted in that direction so I took the opportunity to lean in and be sick. Thereafter, I see-sawed between heads and cooker, but eventually passed the mugs of coffee up to the cockpit, more or less intact. The movement made sleep impossible for all except the very young, for it was difficult to stay in one's bunk, but it soon became evident that we were on a clear run, heeled over but fairly steady, and Dickey came below to change and said they had decided to put into Marzamemi, a fishing village with a small protected harbour, just north of Cape Passaro. I went on deck about four a.m. to find the dawn breaking, and the teenagers gradually emerged, bleary-eyed, to watch the sun rise; as we dropped anchor and started tidying away the sails, two tunny boats came in and dropped anchor near us. The men hailed us cheerfully and rowed over to present us with a large box of herrings. Since they were alongside us all morning, contentedly smoking and waving to us, there was nothing for it but to gut the whole boxful. John said, incautiously, that he knew how to gut fish, so we gave him the box and a knife and told him to go forward and start. Somehow a boat was hailed, and Dickey and the Woods went ashore; the morning became very hot and John was becoming cross, so when Dickey returned with the dinghy, he handed over to Leslie and went ashore with the others.

Anne & Ruth relaxing on Lucette: Malta 1968

While Leslie laboured, I started to wash down the deck, clearing off the fish heads and guts, and became so engrossed that I found myself washing out the cockpit as well. When the others returned all was neat and clean, and we had put the fish into large empty water-bottles, topped up with seawater, in the hope that this would preserve them (it didn't, and the bottles had to go, too), and were frying herrings in egg and oatmeal. To my dismay, none of my family would eat them - I found, subsequently, that they thought it was tunny, which they disliked - the Woods had one each, and Brian and I valiantly ate till we were bursting, for they were delicious. Before departing for Malta again, we had the unpleasant task of cleaning the anchor and chain, as we slowly winched it up, of a ton of primeval slime, and the foredeck had to be cleaned all over again; but we were soon off into a spanking breeze and a glorious fresh sunny day, and the weather continued so all the way home.

The next day Leslie, on washing-up duty, cast our second bucket into the deeps, and we did a man overboard drill to rescue it, which manoeuvre was somewhat complicated by everyone pointing at a different wave. The teenagers became restless after lunch, asking anxiously about our time of arrival, and even more anxiously about Dickey's navigation, pointing out that one would be hard put to miss Sicily, but Malta was very small, and did we have enough food and water to last us to North Africa? Dickey said, patiently, that Malta would appear at three o'clock or thereabouts, and they gathered on the fore hatch, eyes shaded and with much checking of watches. After a while, Dickey added that Malta was often obscured by a heat-haze until one was about three miles off, but they chose to regard this as an escape clause and expressed scepticism. Suddenly, the air thinned in front of us and there was Malta, hazy in the sunshine, about three miles off, and our harbour entrance dead ahead. The children burst into relieved laughter and started chattering cheerfully; the weather was glorious, we were creaming in, all sails set, and three other yachts came out to meet us, hailing us as they came abreast:

"You look marvellous!" one shouted, and we laughed and waved - by golly, we felt marvellous.

As we unloaded, Leslie dropped Roddy's torch overboard. Later, as I blissfully wallowed in a hot bath, Dickey asked, "Did you enjoy it?"

"Well... ", I said, hesitatingly.

"You never like doing the things I like doing!" said Dickey indignantly.

During our three years in Malta, Lucette became a part of our lives, clearly distinguishable from the other yachts as she sailed past our house. A constant rival for Dickey's attention, he spent hours working on her, painting, anti-fouling, fiddling with her engine, her radio, fussing about with her sails, scrounging bits here and there to add to her. We left Malta on the opening day of the first Middle Sea Race, which Dickey had helped to plan and expected to enter; and when we next heard of his dearly-loved Lucette, she had been sunk in the

Pacific by killer whales[17]. She was almost indestructible: Fate certainly gave her a bizarre ending.

---

[17] In 1971, the Robertson family set sail from Cornwall on a round-the-world voyage in their boat Lucette and were capsized by killer whales in the Pacific Ocean. The family survived for six weeks while lost at sea.

Debs Down Under - Australia 1970

When I answered the phone I heard Dickey say "Check the diary for the tenth, would you?"

"All clear that day", I said.

"Oh good, then we can fly Rusty and Eleanor to Cowra for the Debs' Ball"

"What?"

"Tell you when I get home" he said, and rang off.

I got out the map of New South Wales and looked up Cowra. It wasn't far from Canberra, where Dickey was working at the British High Commission in a military capacity, about two hundred miles north of us, on the western slopes of the Great Dividing Range, and two hundred miles from Sydney; about an hour away by single-engine aeroplane, with Dickey as pilot. Browsing over the map, I could see that it wasn't far from my childhood home in Orange, and was probably the same kind of small market town, though Orange had expanded considerably since my schooldays, and I expected that Cowra had done the same. I discovered later that the population numbered about seven thousand.

Recalling my childhood brought to mind Dickey's reference to a Debs' Ball, and I could remember seeing photographs of similar functions in Orange's local paper. Pretty girls in foamy white dresses, formal with gloves and flowers, being presented to a Guest of Honour. I'm not Australian and my previous stay had been brief, so I wasn't sure what it was all about, but later discovered that various churches liked to 'bring out' their seventeen year-old daughters in this fashion.

Presently Dickey arrived and enlarged on the sketchy information provided earlier: the dignitaries of the Protestant Church in Cowra had decided that, this particular year being the bicentenary of Captain Cook's arrival in Australia, it might be fitting if a member of the Royal Navy was invited to attend their ball as Guest of Honour. Accordingly, they contacted the British High Commission and Rusty, Dickey's naval colleague, had received the invitation. Dickey had heard him puzzling over the distance involved (for Rusty had only recently arrived) and had offered to fly him there, provided that pilot and wife could attend the ball in order to observe that humourist in the rather pompous role required of him, for Rusty had a puckish sense of fun and a great deal of cool cheek.

I agreed enthusiastically, and booked myself a shampoo and

set, determined to have my hair swept up in the most formal fashion suitable to the occasion and, when the day of departure arrived, I gave very definite instructions to the hairdresser: "Up on top, and it must be *firm*." And firm it was, apparently set with cement; not being blessed with thick, luxuriant hair, my head appeared to be crowned with a birdcage. When Dickey saw me, he looked thunderstruck:

"I don't like that" he said, incautiously.

Since I was already beginning to regret my rash choice, this remark caused deep offence and we drove to the airfield in dignified silence. Rusty and Eleanor presently joined us and gazed at my hair in amazement. Rusty said kindly that he didn't think it was "quite you, dear". Eleanor agreed with him and I became truculent:

"It's stuck now," I said, "*Nothing* will bring it down!"

This last was soon proved to be true for, as we ran to the aeroplane in a sudden thunderstorm, Rusty opened his umbrella for us and hooked it into my birdcage, which remained as flawless as if carved from rock. After some altercation we climbed into the aeroplane, roared down the runway and set a course for Cowra.

The country unrolled beneath us like a relief map - red soil, grey-green gum trees, a glint of light where a grazier had dammed some water for his stock; the rain spattered against us and the aircraft shook a little in the wind, steadying as Dickey adjusted the trim. Eleanor said something, but I couldn't hear above the engine noise. I cupped my hand round my ear and she shouted, "I don't like this!"

"Have you been in a light aircraft before?" I asked, and she shook her head. I could sympathise: my first trip in a similar aeroplane reduced me to tears of terror!

Aerial view of Cowra: Australia, 1970.

We passed over the edge of the high plateau and the first gorges of the Blue Mountains, thickly clad in green, opened under us, their depths sharply shadowed as we flew out of the storm into sunlight. The sun was low in the sky when we reached the tiny airstrip at Cowra, gilding the small group of cars gathered there, the huddle of men near them casting a long, solid shadow. As we landed and taxied up to them, we noted a gentleman with a clerical collar, and clambered out with as much dignity as we could muster. The men moved slowly forward, a little shy - perhaps they feared that British officers and their ladies would be a little pompous - but Rusty and Dickey soon had us all at ease and laughing, and without further ado Eleanor and I were whisked round to the motel with the baggage, and our husbands were driven off at speed to the golf club, "For a little drink, won't be long!"

As we made ourselves tea in my room, the thunderstorm we had left behind broke over our heads yet again; the day grew dark, lightning flashed and, amid reverberating crashes of thunder, I started shaking out my evening clothes.

"Here," I said, handing Eleanor a pair of white gloves, "I thought you might need these." She stared at me incredulously:

"What for?"

"Well, I remember when I was a child, these affairs were rather formal." Eleanor waved them away.

"That was *then*," she said grandly, "and anyhow, I only wear gloves when the Queen is present!"

I was impressed by this magnificent line. Feeling somewhat crushed, I hastily pushed the gloves back in my case. Indeed, I was so overawed that I put mine back as well.

It was a very long time before Dickey and Rusty returned, and when they finally arrived they were decidedly giggly; we were already dressed and hurriedly helped them into their Mess kit and waited for the car to collect us. There was a thunderous knock at the door, and we opened it onto pitch darkness and wind-lashed rain.

"Come on!" cried the gentleman outside, "Run!"

We picked up our long skirts and ran like mad things down the main street to the vicarage, the men running alongside and holding umbrellas. There were to be drinks for the dignitaries in the vicarage beforehand, apparently, and Eleanor and I galloped through the front door, gasping and spluttering with laughter; as I caught sight of myself in the hall mirror, I was relieved to note that every hair was still rigidly in place. Representatives from the other churches were already in the room, and we were all somewhat formal over our glasses of sherry and dainty savouries. The Vicar explained to Rusty that we would take our places in the hall, and that each girl would be brought over by her escort to be presented, make her curtsey and retire, after which there would be a speech of welcome, followed by a few words from Rusty, and then the festivities would commence.

At last the call came and we were once more pounding down the main street, skirts hoisted. As we entered the foyer of the hall, we saw that the debutantes were already in position, pretty in white, each on the arm of a young man in a dark suit; in front were a tiny flower girl and a small boy, and ladies were fluttering around them, touching a curl here and twitching a fold there. Every member of the group wore white gloves, even the young men. I avoided Eleanor's eye and folded my bare hands in front of me, resisting an urge to clasp them behind my back. The dignitaries - and us - moved into the main room and crossed to the far side in a stately fashion, applauded by the crowd; my hands felt enormous.

Dickie in parade dress with Ruth: Canberra, 27th April 1970.

The room was packed, as was the gallery above. When we reached the wall opposite, Rusty, Dickey and the committee members began jostling and hissing at each other - apparently Dickey, large and imposing in military scarlet with gold-braided, brass-buttoned waistcoat, had been mistaken for the Guest of Honour. Rusty, smaller and neat in Navy Mess kit and black bow tie, gold rings on his sleeves, kept pushing him firmly aside and saying, "Look here, *I'm* the Guest of Honour!" The guests watched in silent astonishment as we sorted ourselves into formation, the clerical gentlemen at the back, the ladies to their front, Rusty, with Dickey at his elbow, at our head.

The compère, standing on the stage, announced the first debutante. The flower girl and her small escort marched fiercely across to us and lined up beside Rusty, who smiled at them fondly, followed by the first couple, white gloves clasped; as they slowly crossed the hall, the compère described the girl's dress, her prowess at school, her hobbies and ambitions. As she reached Rusty she extended her hand, he clasped her fingertips and she sank to the floor in a deep and graceful curtsey. She looked charming. Rusty obviously thought so too for, feeling that the occasion deserved more from him than a bow and a smile, he bent over her hand, raising it gallantly to his lips, and murmured something to her. She jerked up her head, startled, and teetered, off-balance; her escort stared, aghast; Rusty raised her to her feet and returned her to her escort and they moved off, bemused, to stand in front of the stage while the compère announced the next debutante. Rusty repeated this performance through all fifteen presentations, and finally the couples were all lined up in front of the stage, facing the guests with the glassy-eyed look of those striving not to giggle.

The compère welcomed Rusty with a little speech and the Guest of Honour strode confidently onto the stage to make his reply.

"Ladies and gentlemen," he said loudly, "this occasion puts me in mind of the dilemma faced by Barbara Hutton's seventh husband on his wedding night..." He paused and we stared at him, hypnotised; the hall was deathly silent. Rusty continued blandly:

"...He knows what to do, but not how to make it more interesting!"

Beside me, Eleanor gave a small moan; I stared at the floor, the debutantes' line quivered violently and Dickey snickered. There was a moment's deep hush, and I felt the back of my neck prickling as I sensed the reverend gentlemen behind me. Suddenly, the hall erupted in one great blast of laughter. The debutantes clutched their escorts and shrieked, the clergy leaned against the wall and roared, and we three raised our heads in relief, while the cause of the uproar stood on the stage and smirked. I can't recall what else he said, but he was the lion of the evening from then on, and the formality of the occasion was abandoned for that of a country jamboree, resembling a scene from 'Oklahoma'. Not that the clothing was in any way rustic: the ladies were elegantly gowned and coiffed, Sydney being their normal shopping centre, even though two hundred miles away.

We found a bar upstairs, but most of the guests had provided their own drinks, and everybody had brought picnic hampers, cold roast chickens, sandwiches, risottos, pies, cookies, cakes - we were plied with food and drink. Suddenly, drink in one hand and chicken leg in the other, I was plucked from my seat. "Barn dance!" cried the stranger and, clutching my hand, he hurried me down the stairs into the hall, where the floor was now thickly covered with chalk. The men were forming a huge circle, ladies on the inside, the band was already going at a cracking pace, fiddler bowing like a grasshopper, and we were flung into action - I was whirled from one man to another, dizzily racing round and round the room, feet skidding wildly on the chalk; once, Dickey whirled me round, laughing, then disappeared again. The world was a spinning eternity of noise, laughter, blurred faces and I was afraid I'd fly off my feet, but someone always managed to catch me. Finally came a comparative hush and my partner steadied and released me. I tottered giddily towards the stairs, dabbing at my streaming face; Eleanor appeared out of the throng, gasping and laughing, but had enough breath left to tell me that my hair was still intact. It seemed to fascinate her. We went back to our group upstairs, where Dickey eventually joined us, asking if we'd noticed that the band were wearing scarlet jackets very similar to his.

"I only realised it," he said, "when someone grabbed my arm and asked me to play 'Happy Birthday To You'!"

"*I* noticed it," said our naval representative. "It's a very common colour this year!"

Regrettably, the rest of the party is a confused memory, although I know that we were offered more food and drink than was good for us. I can recall that Dickey's face grew darker and damper in the most alarming way as the evening progressed, for he danced with all the ladies in turn and his Mess jacket is of very thick wool with a quilted lining. Midnight made an impact on my memory too, when it was announced that the senior debutante would cut the celebration cake, and we all trooped downstairs to watch. It certainly was a magnificent cake, ornately decorated with pink and white icing. The debutante and her escort stood poised, blade in hand and, as we applauded, they made the first incision. At that precise moment, a small grey mouse rushed out from under the tablecloth. The debutante screamed, dropped the knife and clutched at her skirts, and the ladies all followed her lead. The men laughed and cheered and one of them scooped it up and threw it to another, and as the tiny grey body flew from hand to hand, we stopped clutching our skirts and clutched our low-cut bodices instead. Dickey, thoroughly bemused, said:

"How ingenious! But how did you get the mouse into the cake?"

He seemed to think it was some kind of cabaret act. My alarm for myself became anxiety for the terrified small creature being hurled through the air, and Eleanor and I shrieked to Rusty to take it outside. He deftly fielded the mouse, crossed the hall and put it out the back door, cheered on by the crowd. We eventually did a smart trot along the main street to our motel at about four a.m., where I wrapped my 'bird's nest' in a scarf and collapsed, exhausted, into bed.

We were awakened by the arrival of breakfast. Dickey hurriedly dressed and went to phone Canberra for weather information and flight clearance, while I groped blindly for my cup of tea. Reluctantly, I levered myself upright and caught sight of my reflection in the mirror. I was dumbfounded to see that my hair was completely unruffled. Not even bent sideways. I touched it tentatively with my brush, which skated over the surface but made no impression. It looked rather like an edifice of spun sugar, and probably was. I was becoming very tired of it. Defeated, I decided to wait until I got home, where I could stand under the shower until something gave way. Dickey returned to say that thunderstorms were still rolling round the Canberra area, and the airport was not accepting light aircraft until conditions improved.

Keith, one of the reception committee, arrived to drive us to the airstrip and was temporarily floored on learning that we couldn't depart. He gazed out at the golden sunshine, gum leaves swinging and glittering in the light breeze, magpies yodelling from the lawn, and frowned in thought. Suddenly he said, "Did you know there was a Jap POW cemetery here?" We didn't, and were surprised to hear that there had been any Japanese prisoners of war in Australia.

"This was the only one," he said, "but they were convinced that they were in New Guinea and that their own forces were advancing towards them, so they planned a suicide break-out involving the whole camp. One night they got drunk on home-made sake, made for the wire in a yelling mob and climbed over the bodies of their dead comrades piled against the wire. Quite a lot got away. They wandered around the countryside in a fairly peaceful kind of way, but they knocked off a few of our fellows in uniform. All that's left is the cemetery. Would you like to see it?"

Japanese POW camp during WW2: Cowra, Australia.
Image credit: AWM 064284 Australian War Memorial.

We were interested, so he drove us out of Cowra into the rolling grassland beyond. There was a high wire mesh fence all around the cemetery, which contained gravel paths, young slender gum trees, a stone lamp and brass plaques sunk into the ground, each bearing the name of a Japanese soldier in Japanese and English.

"They're not necessarily the right names," Keith said. "I don't know if any of them are. They never gave them, and they always pretended they hadn't known each other prior to their capture, though some of the officers must have done. To save each other's honour, I suppose. They were supposed to fight to the death or kill themselves, rather than be taken prisoner, and were ashamed because they hadn't, especially the officers." The wind sighed over the grass, gently rattling the gum leaves and throwing dancing shadows over the names, and we stood silent, puzzling over this echo of a barbaric age.

Japanese War Cemetery & Gardens: Cowra, Australia.
Image credit: atlasobscura.com

Rusty broke the silence.

"Where are all the ladies today?" he asked.

"Washing up."

"Washing up what?"

"Well, the hall and the plates and glasses and things." We stared at him, amazed.

"But there must have been about four hundred people there!"

"Oh, easily that," he said. "Makes a lot of mess."

"Well," we said, "come on, take us there. They'll need help!"

On arriving at the hall we found the vicar's wife and the ladies of the committee deep in soapsuds, glasses, plates, empty bottles and boxes of rubbish. Eleanor picked up a dishcloth and I began packing glasses into boxes. Rusty collected rubbish and emptied it into containers outside, while Dickey collected bottles and swept the floor of the hall. The ladies, at first surprised, clearly appreciated our help, and some of the men arrived to assist as well. The time went merrily by, full of chatter and bustle, and it seemed no time at all before we were all sitting down, drinking coffee and eating the remains of the debutantes' cake, and we had just reached the stage of "Did you see old so-and-so last night? My word, wasn't he -" when Keith, glancing round the circle, began to laugh.

"It's just struck me," he spluttered. "We've got the Guest of Honour here cleaning up after the party, and an officer in the Royal Navy at that!"

There was general hilarity for a while, and then a move to the Returned Servicemen's League Club was mooted, so we all scrambled into cars and set off. The RSL, as it is known throughout Australia, vaguely resembles our British Legion. They have clubs in every city and town in Australia and are always busy and thriving centres, often the largest building in a town, with a great deal of money and a powerful voice in the land. They have bars, lounges, a restaurant, billiards room and fruit machines, and most of their members drop in for a quick one on their way home from work. We settled down for a drink before lunch, but our hosts were horrified to learn that our pilot could have no alcohol.

"Eight hours, bottle to throttle," Dickey said firmly.

In between all this driving about, Dickey had been phoning Canberra at intervals, and they eventually relented and allowed us to return. We were escorted to our aeroplane and given an enthusiastic farewell. Fun though it had been, Eleanor and I were anxious to return to our respective children, particularly as Eleanor had a small baby. Her relief at our departure, however, was tempered by her nervousness and, as we neared Goulbourn, our nearest airfield before Canberra, she was alarmed by the severe buffeting we were getting. Dickey decided to land there to check on the weather ahead and, once again, we were told to wait. We waited for two hours, with absolutely nothing to do. It was incredibly boring, and a great relief to climb into the aircraft again for take-off. However, we were tossed around alarmingly as we started to climb, caught in the down-draughts off the sides of the hills, for the ground was rising sharply. Eleanor clutched the back of Rusty's seat and cried "I don't like this, Dickey!" which was the nearest she came to outright rebellion - clearly she would have preferred to walk.

"It's all right," shouted Dickey, "when we gain a bit more height we'll be above the turbulence."

And so it proved, although the aeroplane shuddered and trembled occasionally. Then, ahead, a big navy blue cloud with

Canberra crouching beneath it, and we were sliding down to the runway in a sudden - and, to Eleanor, alarming - silence, as Dickey throttled down and lost airspeed, making a great effort to hold the aircraft steady in the gusty cross-wind. We rolled over to the Flying Club and Dickey shut off the engine.

"Thank you, Dickey," said Eleanor politely. "That was a most interesting experience!"

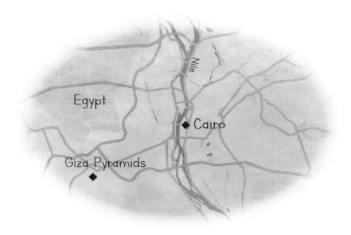

Return to Cairo - Khartoum 1976

Cairo was a disappointment. Twenty-five years ago, when I last saw it, the buildings of the business section looked impressive, the pavements washed clean, Groppis' was the café where everyone met, or watched meetings, over refreshing glasses of fresh lemon, or strawberry ice cream with real crushed strawberries, or Turkish coffee. Now all was seedy, dusty, dirty, the pavements cracked and filthy, buildings with bare brick, no facings, ruts in the road, Groppis' was dirty and peeling and apathetic.

But the pyramids at Giza were just the same, still surrounded by badgering Egyptians: "Take a photo on my camel!", "Take a photo with Arab headdress!", "Take a photo on horse!" Stephanie had to be rescued from their clutches, her instinct to be polite making her easy prey to the practised and avaricious.

Stephanie (& Ruth, partially hidden) at the Giza pyramids:
Cairo, September 1976

The Sphinx was smaller than she expected. We stopped at a wayside café in a small village to buy iced mango-juice with pieces of mango floating in the thick juice, and were immediately surrounded by small children (we were in a Land Rover): "Baksheesh", they coaxed, holding out small cocoa-coloured hands. Flies crawled unnoticed round their huge lustrous black eyes. A small puppy, too young to have left its mother, staggered unsteadily on the dusty ground, missing death by inches, until finally scooped up by the indifferent hands of a girl who flung it in the vehicle window, where it hit the metal floor with considerable force and lay dazed. She then demanded money for it, but our Egyptian driver lifted it out, shouted at the children and drove off.

The Souk, too, was the same as ever: the famous Khan Al-Khalili was there before most of Cairo existed; for many years a thieves' citadel, the police were unable to enter its narrow covered passages, the open ground all around the vast warren gave the occupants ample time to prepare for them. Sometime in the 1920s, a determined police chief managed in some way to out-manoeuvre the opposition and gained access with his force to the sanctuary, and since then all has been peaceful and legal.

Ruth & Stephanie at the Giza pyramids: Cairo, September 1976

And so we wandered past wonderful leatherwork, brass work, copper inlaid with silver, bubbly glass, turquoise and silver jewellery, magnificent kaftans in silk, heavily decorated in gold and silver braid, into the street of gold merchants, wafted along on a thread of musk, gazing at carpets, all in blessed cool shade, the passages wide enough for two people squeezed together.

Then out into the square, meaning to look inside the famous Muhammad Ali Mosque, but it was Friday, the Moslems' holy day, and a service was in progress so we were disappointed.

Ruth, Stephanie & Deirdre[18] with the Land Rover
at the Giza pyramids: Cairo, September 1976

There are many thousands more people now than twenty-five years ago, and the streets are jam-packed with cars, honking, hooting, a clamour of noise, stupefying as a gun barrage. There appear to be no rules, or only very loosely. I was too terrified to watch our progress, as we missed collisions by a miracle, and all at some considerable speed.

---

[18] Deirdre was the wife of the British Military Attaché in Cairo.

Flight to Sennar - Khartoum 1977

When the Eid comes, everything stops for four days. The Souk is shut, the servants gone, and the town and countryside are speckled with gentlemen in snowy white, bulging and fluttering out of buses, or yellow taxis with broken springs and bald tyres, or top-heavy Toyota pickups, or just plodding on foot, white turbans loosened to shade their faces from the broiling sun, visiting, visiting - I don't know how they ever find anyone at home to visit. The wives, of course, don't count. Amazing where they find the strength, for it was a very hot Ramadan this year, the Sudan grilling under the August sun, the house servants rolling their eyes and sighing, Sudanese acquaintances offering one a limp hand and a feeble smile. It will be a hotter Ramadan next year, heaven help them. I hope we'll be on leave.

Actually, the Eid took five days this year, there being some confusion between the priest insisting on seeing the new moon with the naked eye, and the Egyptians insisting on photographing the hair-thin sickle with an electronic camera. Or so the Sudanese say. I'm no technician.

One way and another, it seemed a good time to clear out of Khartoum and do some visiting on our own account. Dennis Leete of Shell Chemicals said we could borrow his aircraft, a Cessna 182, and Bill Hindle said he'd like to go - he's been here twenty-five years, teaching English around the Sudan, and is now head of the English Department at Khartoum Polytechnic. And Bridget de la Billière was keen too. She hasn't been here long, accompanying her husband, Colonel Peter de la Cour de la Billière, late of the Special Air Service, and now heading the British Army Training Team here.

We thought we'd fly down to Sennar, three hundred miles to the south, along the Blue Nile, to visit our landlord, who wants his house back. There being a shortage of accommodation in Khartoum, sweet-talking the landlord is becoming an art form in its own right. Our landlord is a charming old Sudanese gentleman, Hamid Humeida, who owns a cotton factory at Sennar. Difficult to contact because he's often in Rome or London. We then planned to fly west to Kosti on the White Nile, where the Kenana Sugar Estate and factory is still under construction, being built by labourers, artisans and technicians from all over the world.

We took off at 10am, well loaded with cans of British beer for our hosts at Kenana, who had run dry. The rainy season had just finished and the desert was still a faint fuzzy green, covered by a rash of black dots, steadily munching its way through the gauzy verdure and leaving a buff-coloured swathe of desert behind it: the inevitable goats, which could probably turn the green bogs of Ireland into barren wasteland.

The Blue Nile near Khartoum: Sudan, 1977

With the Blue Nile unwinding like a sparkling ribbon beneath us, we flew over the Gezira, an agricultural area between the two Niles, planned and built by the British in the nineteen-twenties, consisting of a series of irrigation canals, fed by the rivers, and rows of fields (to us a patchwork of variegated greens). It is owned by a combine of farmers who pay for the maintenance of the canals, the goat-fencing, fertilizers, hire of crop-dusters and so on, growing cotton, maize, durra and vegetables. We passed over a small airstrip where a neat row of crop-duster aircraft was parked, and presently saw, far below us, a white crop-duster flying to and fro along the strips of green, spraying. He looked like a seagull. I wondered if it was one of the weather-beaten Australian 'croppies' I'd met at the Sudan Club[19]. I hadn't seen any about since I last saw them unconscious by the swimming pool, late one night, surrounded by empty beer cans.

The Gezira gets monotonous after a while and I dozed off, only to be roused by a nudge from Bill, who was sitting beside Dickey, our pilot.

"Do you realise we're all connected with the Loyals[20]?" he asked.

I hadn't, but a moment's reflection brought the matter into focus, thus: Dickey was a Loyal until amalgamation, which includes me; Bill, who came from Preston and was commissioned into the Loyals in the late nineteen-forties and served at Hadrian's Camp, Carlisle, under Brigadier Rimbault; and Bridget is the daughter of Colonel Basil Goode, Loyals.

Wad Medani came into view, and we all craned our necks to see how the Chinese were getting on with their bridge, which spans the Nile at this point. It joins the Khartoum-Wad Medani road to the new road to Kassala on the Eritrean border, where there is almost a new road to Port Sudan. When

---

[19] The British ex-pats' social club in Khartoum
[20] The Loyal (North Lancashire) Regiment

I say 'new', I mean 'virgin'. Wad Medani itself is uninteresting, though it was once a green and thriving town. Beyond it, a red dirt track leads to Sennar, and I was glad to be above and not on it. It's a very good way to loosen your fillings, if not your teeth, travelling on these ungraded dirt tracks. I once did it from Juba to Yei and back in an army lorry, and I lost two fillings and cracked a tooth.

Sennar and its surrounding area looks very much like northern Kenya: red sandy soil, flat acacia trees and round huts with conical thatched roofs. The Blue Nile is dammed here, and we could see the foamy cataract tumbling at the end of the lake. There are crocodiles here, but game is scarce, driven away by huge lorries pounding over the desert, and by spreading habitation. In the centre of the little town was a warren of Arab-style houses, sun-baked bricks or adobe walls, neatly whitewashed, glistening like dry bones. Down by the small strip near the cotton factory a car awaited us. The landlord's 'man', a cousin some hundred times removed, welcomed us politely and drove us to Hamid Humeida's unpretentious house. He came out to greet us, black face beaming, arms spread wide, dressed in dazzling white djellabiya and turban, civet-catskin slippers on his feet.

"Ahlan wasahlan, kayf haalek? Quoisa? Humdilillah!" and ushered us indoors, where we washed our hands as the local custom is, and sat down to fresh lemon juice and tea and polite conversation with Sayed Humeida and his son-in-law, who speaks excellent English. Mohammed, the son-in-law, and

Bill eyed each other covertly. After a pause, Bill said, "I know your face, Mohammed."

"Yes," said Mohammed, "you taught me English at Wad Medani!" Whereupon they fell to reminiscing.

"What happened to 'Quo Vadis'?" asked Bill.

"That's not an Arab name!" I said.

"It was his nickname," said Mohammed, "the Sudanese are very fond of nicknames. They keep them all their lives."

Four visitors came in - men, of course - much hand-shaking and laughter, more tea and some talk of local politics, swapping smoothly from English to Arabic with never a pause; the landlord's wife crept in, shook hands all round and crept out again. A pity, because we had once found her at home alone and had taken the intrepid old lady, who had never been in an aeroplane, for a short flight, after which she asked us the price of the aircraft and decided that they would buy one; I found her a very jolly lady indeed.

After a light lunch, for which our landlord apologised, explaining that after their long fast they ate very little (there was more than we could manage), we made our polite farewells and attempted to leave. Horrors, outside were two large boxes of fresh grapefruit and a huge bunch of bananas. Dickey was forced to explain that we had a weight limit and could carry no more. Our landlord was dismayed, his man clearly appalled.

"We could take two each", said Dickey, desperately.

They loaded our arms with grapefruit and we staggered into

the car, attempting to shake hands and wave without dropping our fruit.

*Ruth, Bridget & Bill clutching fruit from
Hamid Humeida (3rd left): Sennar, 1977*

As we bounced our way along the strip, the passengers realised that it was very short indeed. There was little 'lift' in the heat of the day. Of course, there was a great deal of desert beyond, but the strip was separated from it by a goat fence. However, we lumbered into the air and headed west. This was a new bit of desert to me and I had a good look round; it seemed to be greener than that around Khartoum, with more trees; obviously they had more rain than we did. Ahead, a jebel grew out of the horizon: Jebel Moya, Water Mountain. Hamid Humeida said it had no water, but it was covered in green vegetation, unlike the bare, brown-black jebels in other parts of the Sudan. I heard later that there was a large, empty

Victorian mansion up there, built of huge concrete blocks, with a plaque on it inscribed 'Wellcome. Uribe. 1913'. This puzzled many people, who thought that welcome was misspelt. Someone decided to investigate further recently, and discovered that it had been built by Mr Wellcome, of Burroughs and Wellcome, the pharmaceutical firm, and by a Major Uribe in the year stated. I can't remember why. The British seemed to have a passion for building houses in the Sudan at one time, always somewhere inaccessible.

The red soil below abruptly changed to black, the rich silt of the Blue Nile. This area is the alluvial plain of the Blue Nile, extending almost to the White Nile, ideal for growing sugar. The Blue Nile, however, ceases to water it after the floods, so the nearby White Nile has been harnessed to irrigate the plain. In any case, they are forbidden to tamper with the Blue Nile by an agreement with Egypt. There are huge canals, built up, dug down, reinforced, seepage, drainage, mighty pumps, dams, irrigation canals, capillary canals - it all stretched below us, along with the skeleton of a factory, untidy collections of yellow bulldozers, trucks and the usual paraphernalia of industrial plant, a railway spur, rows of prefabricated houses, and a club with squash courts and a turquoise swimming pool. It all looked as if they were trying to populate the moon. It was 4pm and the shadows were hard black outlines in the sun's glare. We made a bumpy landing, loose stones skittering from under our tyres, and as we stepped out a hot breeze tossed red dust round our ankles. Two pickups awaited us and delivered us to the guesthouse, also prefabricated. Inside, air conditioners throbbed softly, and all was most luxurious. We had cold baths and collapsed until sunset.

After a drink with our hosts we strolled over to the club - very pleasant, but empty.

"No food here", said the barman. "Food over in canteen."

So we made our way to the canteen. It looked like any other canteen: self-service, one half had tables and chairs, the other half counters and open kitchen. The air conditioners struggled, but the heat from the kitchen conquered. Sweat started to trickle down our faces.

"There's a film at eight", said a friendly chap in shorts, checked shirt and red beard. "Showing in here. Sit in front, it's a small screen."

The room was filling with red-skinned, sun-bleached Europeans, Scots, Brits, some washed and changed, most still in the dusty, sweaty, crumpled clothes they'd worn all day. A few women, youngish, some in gay cotton djellabiyas, one or two in very tight jeans, swaying past the yearning gaze of the bored men. As the film progressed, the trickle of sweat became a river and we were glad to move out into the open afterwards.

Lightning flickered along the horizon and there was a faint rumble of thunder; a fitful wind whipped the dead grass round my legs.

"I hope the aircraft's all right", Dickey said.

Sometime in the night the wind freshened, and Dickey went to find a vehicle to take him to the strip. He found a guard room and they obligingly drove him to the aircraft. Two ghaffirs[21] rose from the gloom and assured him that they were watching the aeroplane with the greatest attention. What they intended to do in the event of gales or haboobs[22] was a mystery. Each hang onto a wing? However, the squally weather blew over.

Bill Hindle, Bridget de la Billière, Dickie & Ruth: Kenana, 1977

We made our way to the canteen for breakfast. As we entered, a gust of hot, greasy air hit us. My stomach gave a queasy lurch. Bill and Dickey brought over platefuls of fried bread, fatty bacon, sausages and fried eggs, and I fled for the door and the open air. Later we toured the site in a Range Rover, connected by radio to the site HQ. It was vast. We were like ants creeping along the great waterways. The levees

[21] Night watchmen
[22] Dust storm

were like mountains on either side. The heat was intolerable - to me - and I elected to remain in the shade while the others toiled up the gradients to view the marvels of hydro-engineering.

We waited on the strip to let a Britten-Norman Islander take off. The regular DC3 flight had been in earlier. We circled the site to view from above what had been explained to us on the ground. The site shimmered in shifting waves of hot air. I was glad not to be stationed there, although they get a lot of leave. Bill was in a tizzy to get back to his home-brewed beer.

"It's ready for bottling", he explained.

The local beer is horrible. Bill makes his own, and I hear it's very good. He recently returned from leave to find his ghaffir had sold the lot, and all his empty bottles as well - these last being virtually unobtainable. So he had started afresh.

Once again I dozed over the Gezira, waking as we approached Jebel Aulia - a small jebel beside a big dam on the White Nile, full of fish and fishing birds. I've even seen kite-hawks paddling in the water, fishing, their leg-feathers all bedraggled. Over mud villages and small towns and into Khartoum, a green oasis by the confluence of White and Blue Niles. Bill had left his car at our house, so we left Dickey to put the aeroplane to bed and took a taxi back. The heat was intense. I gave the driver 25 piastres. He gave it back.

"50 piastres", he said.

I looked at the airfield perimeter nearby. We had driven half a mile round it. I gave him back the 25 piastres, walked through the gate and slammed it shut. As I walked in the front door, he was still yelling. I don't know where he found the energy to argue. I'd used up all mine.

Omdurman by the Blue Nile seen from the air: Khartoum, 1978

The Screen Hanging - Khartoum 1976-79

The Rumanian National Day was a surprise. We drove to their Residency. Pitch black (the New Extension[23] had a power cut) and empty. To their embassy. Also black and empty. So where were they? Dickey blamed Ahmed the driver (he should have done his homework), and I suggested Dickey check the invitation (which I hadn't seen). He said it was at home. So we went home. It was in the office and locked up and the phone was dead. He'd only glanced at it but had a feeling it said something about the Sudan Socialist Union Club. So we drove round there. The cars were all there but no sound of festivities, and the front of the building was dead. So we scrunched on the gravel drive and looked round the back.

---

[23] A modern suburb of Khartoum

The garden was brilliantly floodlit. Rows and rows of chairs faced a stage (and us) and rows and rows of eyes turned towards us. Not a familiar face did I recognise. On the stage, a lady (Sudanese) was making a speech. She stepped down. Applause. A tall Sudanese made a long speech. Applause. The lady came back and spoke. Applause. It was hot under the arc lights and we were being attacked by flies and things. The Rumanian ambassador made a long, boring, cliché-ridden political speech including the catch-phrase "we must make the Israelis return the territory they have stolen". Applause. No-one else was in evening dress or uniform excepting Dickey and I. The lady came back and spoke. Applause. No-one brought any drinks or snacks. A little fat Sudanese with a breathy tenor voice made a long speech, but a diversion was supplied by six Sudanese trying to erect a cinema screen behind him, in perfect silence, accompanied by sign language.

They tried to close the shutters on the French windows behind the speaker and this was quite amusing, for the shutter was white and the long striving fingers appearing through the slots were black. Then they appeared in front, but couldn't hang the screen high enough. They had no ladder. One brought a chair. He balanced two chair legs on the step and held up the other side. Another climbed upon it and raised the screen, which was meanwhile being rolled up and unrolled apparently at the whim of a solid gentleman in a white suit. At last, satisfied, they stood back to admire the results. It was hanging squint and was only partially visible to the operator.

Back to the chair and the unrolling. Two others carried in a table, whilst another bit through an electric flex with his huge creamy teeth. He bit through it twice and produced a piece with which to tie up the screen. What the flex was for originally was a mystery. It wasn't for the loud-speakers, for our lecturer continued to drone on.

Still in silence, someone stood on the table and, whilst the speaker lavished praise on President Nimeiry, they carefully hung the screen over the president's portrait and made it fast to the portrait's picture hook. They picked up table and chair and unhurriedly left the stage. They had made no sound throughout their performance - I had great difficulty in keeping a straight face. The speaker finished and left the stage and, as the applause rang out, we rose silently from our seats and scrunched away. All the speeches were in Arabic except the ambassador's. Quite a collection of diplomats escaped with us, following Dickey like a fleeing army. We had our drink and snack at home.

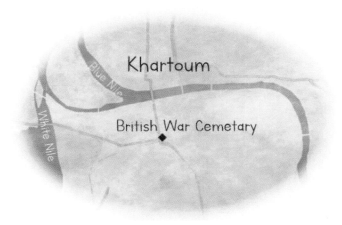

Funeral in Khartoum - Khartoum 1977

Living in the Sudan has much in common with opening an old trunk in the attic and riffling through its dusty contents: yellowed newspapers, dog-eared books, bundles of letters with faded, once-familiar handwriting, recalling faces and voices long gone. The Sudanese have long memories, and men they have admired remain in their conversation... "That was when Mr Brown was headmaster at Hantoub", I have often heard. The old silversmith in Omdurman, who once gave me his visiting card inscribed 'Ahmed Suleiman Silver and Smith', said he could remember Kitchener. He mentioned it every time I went into his shop to look at his silver, no doubt assuming that I, too, knew Kitchener.

But not all the memories are second-hand. Some of them belong to the old residents, the foreigners, now tucked away in odd corners of that vast land, perfectly adjusted to their environment and happy among the friendly Sudanese. Just such a character was Fred March.

The old silversmith in Omdurman. Drawing by Anne Bird

I never met old Fred, but when we heard that there was an old Australian living in austere circumstances in Khartoum, Dickey hurried off to see that all was well, for he has a fondness for Australians and, besides, there was no Australian Embassy in Sudan. He gave me the details on his return.

Fred was ninety-four. He'd gone to Gallipoli with the ANZAC Brigade in the First World War, and earned the Military Medal by swimming among mines and cutting them adrift from the sea-bed. He didn't go home with the Anzacs and his next public appearance was as the British Resident's chauffeur in Cairo during the 1920s. The British Resident was a Very Important Person in those days and it seemed that he was in some disfavour with the populace, because one day his car was surrounded by a Riotous Mob. This is not unusual in Cairo and mostly results in burning trams and smashed shop windows, but someone in the crowd opened fire on the stationary car and made a hole in the British Resident. He made a few in Fred, too, who accelerated into the crowd and drove his late boss to hospital. Fred survived to be awarded the Albert Medal, which later became the George Medal. After that, Fred drifted down to the Sudan and took a clerical post in the Ministry of Agriculture until he retired. He spoke vaguely of different wives of various nationalities, but was now married to Teresa, a shy little Eritrean some years his junior. No, he didn't mind the austerity of his life, but he did miss cornflakes. And whisky.

And so we gave him the odd packet of cornflakes and an occasional bottle of whisky. Unbeknown to us, other members of the British Embassy were also surreptitiously performing this same small favour. A year later, Fred passed on, probably from a surfeit of cornflakes and whisky.

It was high summer when he died and Teresa couldn't think who to contact. She knew it should be the British Consul, but he was laid low in the Khartoum Clinic and too ill to be of help. Eventually, she was directed to the Vice Consul, David. David bustled efficiently round to the morgue, accompanied by one of his henchmen, and there he received a series of nasty shocks. The first was that the morgue was unpleasantly hot. The second was that there were no undertakers in the Sudan. The third was that *he* would have to prepare the body for burial. He couldn't believe it. He drove round to the British Chaplain (a New Zealander, actually, with an Australian wife) who said, "I only bury them." But Mrs British Chaplain had been a nurse and had often prepared bodies for burial, and said they would need a winding sheet and a shroud. David thanked her profusely and said, in that case, would she...? No, she said firmly, she was pregnant and couldn't. However, she would go to the Souk and buy some local unbleached cotton and make up the items required.

David went back to the embassy to report, and Dickey heard the news and said that Fred would have to have a military funeral. David ordered the embassy carpenter to make a coffin immediately, and Dickey sent messages to the members of the British Army Training Team in Omdurman (it was always impossible to contact them by phone). The BATT contained five officers and three warrant officers, and the British Embassy provided a major and warrant officer besides Dickey. A bugler was promised from the Sudanese armed forces, plus an NCO[24] to advise him. Dickey rushed home to change into uniform. The red band round his cap glowed in the throbbing sunlight and perspiration trickled from under it, running down his face. He was carrying a coil of climbing robe.

---

[24] Non-commissioned officer: probably, in this instance, a corporal or a sergeant

"What's that for?" asked a startled friend.

"I'm taking it to a funeral", he explained.

"Are you going to bury him or hang him?" queried our visitor.

At 3pm they assembled in the church and waited for the funeral cortège. Nothing happened for a very long time. To go back a little, David had collected the items required from Mrs British Chaplain and returned to the morgue. He felt ill at ease. Well, he felt *ill*. But like a true son of Albion he completed his task, and they nailed down the lid and bent to lift the box. The wood was extremely heavy and they couldn't get it off the floor. Summoning assistance, they wearily tottered up the stairs and into the blast furnace of day.

Dickie in uniform by the pool at home: Khartoum 1978

There was no sign of the hearse, so they stood in the shade of the doorway and waited. After fifteen minutes David became desperate and waved down a passing 'box-car'. These are Toyota pick-ups, converted to carry passengers in the back, and they ply for hire around Khartoum. This one had one passenger, and he and the driver were delighted by this variation in their daily routine. They enthusiastically loaded the coffin aboard and insisted on accompanying the funeral party to church, beaming with pleasure.

The congregation, melting and wondering, were relieved to see things under way at last, and the service went on without any further trouble. Until the end, that is, when they all followed the coffin to the door. *It* went through but they didn't, for the Chaplain shooed them all back to their pews and announced another hymn. Puzzled, they obliged, but when it faltered into silence they were urged to remain and, disciplined to the last, sat fast. Eventually, there was the unmistakable sound from outside of a hubcap being kicked into place, and the Chaplain released them. Outside, David explained that the hearse had arrived at the church with a flat tyre. The spare was also flat, so the driver had borrowed the Chaplain's bicycle, slung the tyre over his shoulder and wobbled off to the nearest garage to affect a temporary repair. David was becoming a little tense and was speaking through clenched teeth.

They followed the hearse to the cemetery, where the Sudanese bugler and attendant NCO awaited them. There was a row of trees down the side of the cemetery near the grave, and they all crowded under them. The Chaplain peered into the hole.

"It's not deep enough", he said accusingly.

David had a look. No, it wasn't deep enough.

"I can't be *everywhere*, he said, "*I* had to prepare the body!"

The Chaplain gazed at him and made no reply. He stared round at the small group of uniforms. They straightened up and stared back with great dignity. The original gravediggers were not in sight. The ground was like cement and the sun was a ball of fire above his head.

"Come on!" he snarled at his assistant and, finding the appropriate tools in a nearby hut, they climbed into the hole. The bugler and the NCO watched them with great interest from the shade of a neem tree, the military mopped their streaming faces and the Chaplain murmured comfortingly to Teresa. Eventually he took another look into the hole.

"That'll do", he said.

David, a deep puce, clambered feebly out. His assistant was Sudanese and didn't appear to be troubled by the heat. The climbing rope was slipped round the coffin and it was lowered into place. The bugler blew gently into his bugle and the NCO raised a restraining hand, watching Dickey, who had stiffened to attention. The Chaplain raised his book, opened it at the marker and drew breath. Then he leant forward to look at the coffin. Frowning, he turned to David.

"Which way is his head?" he asked.

Silently, David pointed.

"He's the wrong way round", said the Chaplain.

"*He* doesn't know that!" bawled David, beside himself with frustration and exhaustion.

"You'll have to take it out and turn it round", said the Chaplain decisively, "that's the rule." He shut his book with a snap and turned his back.

Khartoum War Cemetery: 1977

Pop-eyed with fury, teeth clenched to splinter point, David dragged his assistant over and they painstakingly raised the coffin again. The bugler, who had been standing with the bugle to his lips, breath drawn, eyes rolled round in Dickey's direction, lowered his instrument and glanced questioningly at the NCO, who shrugged. Carefully, the coffin was turned and lowered again. Teresa watched quietly, perfectly used to a life of confusion and uncertainty, and sure that the British would get it right in the end. Satisfied, the Chaplain completed the service, the bugler, thoroughly perplexed, played his part with gusto and the mourners dispersed, wilting and weary. Except for Teresa, who was very pleased. Fred would have been pleased too, but for different reasons.

When I went to pay my respects some days later, a rough wooden cross had been erected over the grave. On it was painted 'Frederic Marsh'. Fortunately, the Consul had planned for this funeral in advance, and when he emerged from the Clinic he had the remains moved to the British Military Cemetery next-door, cared for by the War Graves Commission. Over the grave is a handsome stone on which is engraved 'Frederick March, GM, MM. RIP'.

Hello Sailor! - Khartoum 1976-79

Nice to see the Royal Navy joining us in the 'Lad'[25], not only because they're good company, but also because it shows us that behind the smart turn-out and glamorous ports of call, there are weeks of boredom, repetitive duties and physical discomfort. There's no closer tie than shared suffering.

I know a naval gentleman who suffered a lot in the cause of duty. My unsuspecting friend had congratulated himself on landing the job of Naval Attaché Cairo. It sounded exotic and not too energetic. Part of his parish was Sudan, of course, but

---

[25] Dickie's Regimental Journal, *The Lancashire Lad* (here shortened to the *Lad*) had just announced that HMS Active had recently become officially linked to his regiment. This story was published in *The Lancashire Lad*. Since everyone except Ruth spelt his name Dickie, her usual spelling of his nickname was changed by the *Lad*'s Editor.

there was only one port there. His only duties in Sudan involved welcoming visiting ships of the Royal Navy, arranging entertainment during their stay and attending their departure. Anything else could easily be dealt with by the Defence Attaché in Khartoum, one Colonel Bird. The general air of imminent collapse and frenetic chaos that hung over Cairo must have alarmed him a little, to say the least, on his arrival there.

Sudan Airways billboard: Khartoum 1978

Another disagreeable matter was finding that the Sudanese government insisted that anyone flying from Cairo to Khartoum on government business had to fly with Sudanair. Sudanair requires a little explanation…

For a start, it didn't always leave when it said it would, and it sometimes did when it said it wouldn't. Sometimes it let passengers get to the foot of the steps only to order them back to the departure lounge while it loaded Ministers with urgent government business, then filled the remaining seats with passengers apparently picked at random. Above all, it never *ever* told you what was going on.

Travelling Sudanair was a lottery all right, and Commander X was no gambler. Besides, changing flights on the same airline was definitely a form of Russian roulette. So he was delighted to find that the Defence Attaché in Khartoum could perform a personal air-taxi service for the 900 mile hop over the mountains to Port Sudan *and* put him up in a comfortable house in Khartoum into the bargain. Staying at the hotel in Port Sudan gave him a severe cultural shock.

All went smoothly, more or less, until one day the world fell on him. The Minister for the Navy was about to pay him a visit (and Egypt as well). At about the same time Commander X had to meet a Royal Navy ship visiting Alexandria and then rush down to Port Sudan to meet another Royal Navy ship. If he hit the ground running at Port Sudan, he just had time to shout hello and then dash back to Cairo to meet the Boss. But if Sudanair did a funny on him, he was sunk. A frantic telephone call to the DA in Khartoum caused further anxiety, because his air-taxi pilot was grounded by a visitor from MOD[26], one Colonel Y. The DA booked him on the Sudanair flight connection and presumably breathed the magic words 'Government Minister' over the wire because Commander X

---

[26] Ministry of Defence

arrived, was briefed over a coffee and departed on time (about 3pm), having also been booked on the 'breakfast' flight back from Port Sudan.

The British Defence Attaché's residence in Khartoum: December 1976.

That evening we took Colonel Y with us to a farewell dinner where the host was generous with his liqueurs and brandy. We got home very late; the two gentlemen somewhat anaesthetised by brandy fumes. We escorted Colonel Y to his room, which opened out onto the wide verandah at ground level, so that we could explain about anti-burglar precautions. I closed the wooden shutters, locked them with a stout bicycle chain and handed the key to the Colonel, telling him not to put it where it could be reached by a hooked stick through the shutter. We slept upstairs under the stars on a roofless wide balcony. Dickie fell instantly asleep and I only paused to put in my earplugs (the noise of pi-dogs[27] fighting in the streets was inclined to cause insomnia) before doing the same.

Around 2.30am Commander X drove up to our front gate in a taxi and had a loud altercation with the driver. This woke our night watchman, who joined in. Having dealt with the driver, Commander X crunched his way round to the back of the house where he knew we would be sleeping. Encouraged by the night watchman he called softly. Then louder. Soon he found that he was screaming at the top of his voice. Not even the policemen guarding the American ambassador next-door-but-two stirred. The night watchman indicated that another Inglesi was sleeping in the garden bedroom, so he scrunched back around the house to the front verandah. Here he tapped politely on the shutter.

Colonel Y was deeply asleep, lulled by the hum of the air conditioner and brandy fumes. There was a pounding in his head and a voice screaming in the distance. He floated up to consciousness and realised that there were men kicking the shutters and shouting. Burglars, no doubt, trying to get in. Fancy asking him to open the door!

"Go away", he mumbled, "You can't come in!"
But the voice continued fading in and out as he dozed off and reawakened. He didn't know how long it was before he realised that the shouter outside was English. He tottered over

---

[27] A term used to describe an ownerless, half-wild, free-ranging dog that lives in or close to human settlements throughout Asia. Ruth picked up the expression in Borneo and Malaya, and never forgot it.

to the shutter and tried to make sense out of the noise. After a while he decided to let the fellow in. But he couldn't find the key. It eventually appeared on the dresser. Trying to get a key into a bicycle chain padlock is a fiddly task and Colonel Y made a poor job of it. It fell onto the tiled floor and skittered under the wardrobe.

"That's it!" he said, and went back to bed.

How it came about that he later let Commander X in the front door neither of them could explain.

Through my earplugs I heard a faint shrieking. Half opening my eyes I saw a figure bending over Dickie, shaking him up and down and yelling at him. The Navy whites[28] were Persil-white in the moonlight. Interested, I eased out an earplug.

"Give me my ticket!" the figure bawled. "Give me my ticket! My flight leaves at 7am! Give me my ticket!"

"What are you doing back here?" mumbled Dickie, his voice distorted by the bouncing his head was getting.

"I got the same aircraft back after turnaround in Port Sudan. Wake up! Give me my ticket!"

"There's no flight until 11am", Dickie said, his voice rising, "and the Embassy's locked until 7am and your ticket's in my office! Go to bed".

"No, no! They told me at the airport! It's leaving at 7am and I've got to be on it!"

This little bit of business was being conducted at full volume in the open air in the middle of the night. Even the dogs had

---

[28] Royal Navy tropical dress uniform

stopped barking. They were probably listening too.

"They'll tell you anything at the airport", Dickie snapped. "The Embassy is sealed until 7am and you can't get your ticket until then. Go to bed: I'll take you in at 7am".

Commander X flung up his hands in exasperation and disappeared, presumably to bed.

He was back at 6am, fidgety with impatience. I waved a cheery greeting and said how crisp and fresh he looked and what would he like for breakfast. He declined, saying he'd eat on the flight, at which I laughed heartily. Muttering, Dickie got the car out and they roared off, getting to the Embassy at 7am, collecting the ticket and depositing the Commander at the airport. We were having breakfast an hour later when we heard him arguing with another taxi-driver outside the gate. He came in, looking weary and dejected.

"There's no-one there", he said, "Just a chap who said the flight didn't leave until 11am".

I'm sorry to say that we three roared with laughter and then became very witty at the unfortunate Commander's expense. Poor chap, he looked a broken man. You can't plan things in third world countries: you can only pray. Commander X must have had a powerful prayer, for he got back in time to greet the Minister at Cairo airport. It's not all gold braid and gin, being a Naval Attaché.

Photo gallery

Ruth (aged 5): Aberdeen 1937

Ruth (centre, aged 5) & shipboard friends at Marseilles en route to Borneo on board P&O liner Corfu: November 1937.

Ruth (aged 15): Suez 1947

A view from the flat: Trieste 1952

Ruth by the dressing table in the bedroom: Trieste, 1952

Dickie (far left) & Ruth (3rd right) at the Warrant Officers'
& Sergeants' Christmas Ball: Trieste, 1952

Ruth (4 months pregnant with Leslie) in village of Villa Opicina:
Trieste, September 1953

Ruth & Leslie at Gibraltar Barracks, Lazzaretto,
by the Adriatic Sea: Trieste, July 1954

Anne & Leslie wearing pinafore dresses made by Ruth:
Camberley, England 1958

Ruth, Tigne & Stephanie inspecting the fishing fleet: Malta, 1967

*Lt Col Geoff Dockerill, Dickie's Commanding Officer,
& Ruth on the Nicholson: Malta, 1968*

Ruth & Dickie on Lake Burrinjuck, NSW: Australia, March 1970

Stephanie, Beryl & Frank Hubbard¹, Ruth & Leslie at Mount Top, Euchareena, NSW: Australia, September 1970

Ruth & her escort at the Zaire border during an official trip of Dickie's to Juba: Sudan, 1977

Stephanie & Ruth buying baskets at Roseires Dam on the Blue Nile south of Khartoum: Sudan, 1978

Ruth & Sudanese fishermen at Jebel Aulia reservoir: Khartoum, December 1976.

Ruth at the Merowe pyramids: Sudan 1976 – 79.

photoMemoirs

This book is published by Photomemoirs.co. Anyone can write a photo memoir without any writing skills. Photomemoirs is an easy and fun way to do it. To get started, order the Photomemoirs instruction pack. Then find your most memorable photographs and record their story in your own words - as if you were showing them to someone and sharing your memories. Send us the photos and recordings and we will make your book! The concept of Photomemoirs is to be more than a photo album, but less than an autobiography. To sign up visit the website www.Photomemoirs.co